WOMEN &

FASHION

A NEW
LOOK

WOMEN &

FASHION

A NEW LOOK

QUARTET BOOKS
LONDON   NEW YORK

CAROLINE EVANS & MINNA THORNTON

First published in Great Britain by Quartet Books Limited 1989
A member of the Namara Group 27/29 Goodge Street, London W1P 1FD

British Library Cataloguing in Publication Data

Evans, Caroline
Women & Fashion: a new look
1. Women's clothing. Fashion
I. Title   II. Thornton, Minna
746.9'2

ISBN 0-7043-2691-4

Typeset by MC Typeset, Gillingham, Kent
Originated by York House Graphics, Hanwell
Printed and bound in Great Britain by Hazell Watson & Viney Ltd, Aylesbury, Bucks

FOR OUR FAMILIES, OUR FRIENDS
AND ESPECIALLY FOR CALUM AND GARY.

TABLE OF CONTENTS

REFERENCES

Books and articles are referred to in the text by the author's surname followed by the date of publication. The full title, publisher and place of publication are given in the Bibliography.

ACKNOWLEDGEMENTS

We would like to thank Leslie Dick, who combined a keen critical eye with enthusiasm and encouragement when we needed it; without her invaluable contribution this would have been a very different book. We cannot thank her enough.

Many other friends helped with ideas, books, or enthusiasm, made useful suggestions, or read sections of the manuscript. They are Rick Ball, Peter Campbell, Paul McAlinden, Joe Staines, Gary Stevens, Calum Storrie, Drake Stutesman, Ann Thornton, Dora Thornton, Peter Thornton, Peter Wollen.

Gina Birch, Sophie Richmond, Simon Withers, Ted Polhemus, Lynn Proctor and Anne Wichard helped us enormously with anecdotes and information. Yuki Maekawa of Comme des Garçons gave her time as generously as she did information and photographs. We would also like to thank Alex Kroll of Condé Nast without whose help it would not have been possible to use many of the pictures in this book. Madeleine Ginsberg and Avril Hart of the Victoria and Albert Museum also helped with pictures. Many of the individual photographers whose work we used were helpful and generous.

Finally we would like to thank the library staff at the London College of Fashion and at St Martin's School of Art, Jane Hoy, Mary Kennedy and the women's studies students at the University of London's Department of Extra Mural Studies, and especially the fashion students at St Martin's.

FOREWORD

When we started to write this book the working title was *Feminism and Fashion*. We rapidly realized that it was never intended to be a book about feminism so much as a book informed by feminism – in other words, a New Look at an old subject that has been dealt with from almost every other point of view.

The late 1980s seems a particularly appropriate time in which to undertake this project. The urgency of the demands of the early Women's Liberation Movement has given way to a multiplicity of feminisms. What is loosely called 'theory' – ideas coming out of post-structuralism and the specifically feminist appropriation of psychoanalytic theory – has provided a framework for a multiplicity of approaches. From this perspective it is possible to rework the old ideas associated with women's interest in fashion, such as vanity, frivolity and triviality, ideas that have been used to castigate both women and fashion. A fundamental part of this project has been our re-evaluation of feminine narcissism, femininity and the marginal, and female masquerade.

While we believe that it is inappropriate to talk about 'post feminism' where this implies that the goals of the Women's Movement have been achieved, the change of emphasis in current feminism allows for a reading which is, we hope, theoretical but not doctrinaire, and which can focus specifically on the relation of femininity and fashion, an issue which in the past has been, so to speak, too hot to handle.

In the following chapters we have tackled the questions which we found most interesting and which seemed to be the most urgent. Each area required a different address, different analytical tools, and different points of reference. The result is a heterogeneous discussion of women and fashion which makes several different kinds of appeal to the reader. We can imagine many different readers, even a different reader for each chapter. Neither a comprehensive history of fashion, nor an all-encompassing critique, the book makes sense and coheres as a collection of essays. For example, Chapter 1, 'Feminism, Fashion, Femininity', is about history and polemics, whereas Chapters 6 and 7 focus on design, specifically in relation to five women designers, and Chapter 5 looks at fashion imagery in terms of current theories of representation.

On the whole the book ignores conformism and reaction in fashion. These are certainly areas which need to be discussed, but in our search for new ways to think about fashion we have been drawn, in the first instance, to those practices which are radical, demanding or critical. The book is explicitly analytical; it is, on the whole, about images and ideas in fashion, rather than about cut and fit.

Within the heterogeneity of our approach a consistent element has been our wish to explore, rather than to assume, the relation of women to fashion. The book is an inquiry on several levels into what that relation might be, and as such it challenges any account which assumes a relation of women to fashion as given, either in theory or in practice. More conventional accounts of fashion generate and maintain a discourse in which the identification of fashion with women and with femininity goes unquestioned. Here we use feminist perspectives to examine the terms of that identification, focusing on existing discourses about fashion and its representations.

Simultaneously, we have tried to suggest the terms of a different kind of debate about fashion. The intellectual or theoretical basis for our treatment is something like a patchwork, in which we have eclectically stitched together disparate practices, texts, theories, arguments and attitudes. We have tried to establish a basis on which an analysis and appreciation of women's fashion could be combined with sexual and cultural politics. Inevitably, and perhaps fashionably, the seams show. While working on the book we rarely felt we were on solid ground, which made it both difficult and exciting.

We think of this book as something of a first exercise of its kind. There are a great many important matters which are beyond its scope. In discussing fashion at the level of representation the book does not analyse fashion in terms of particular political issues, economics or sociology. We hope that the following chapters will contribute to studies of women's fashion which refer specifically to issues of *social* marginalization, issues of race, class and sexuality – studies which we know, in some cases, are already being written. Here we have focused on fashion as a discourse which is *culturally* marginalized within the hierarchies of art and of history. It is precisely as a culturally marginalized practice that fashion can utter those meanings which are both compelling and oblique.

The book is a preliminary study which maps out a field of inquiry and indicates how it might be further explored. Ultimately we want the following discussion of women and fashion to work to free the ways in which women might appropriate fashion and its representations. Fashion is a field in which women have found pleasure in the elaboration of meaning – meaning which is there to be taken and used.

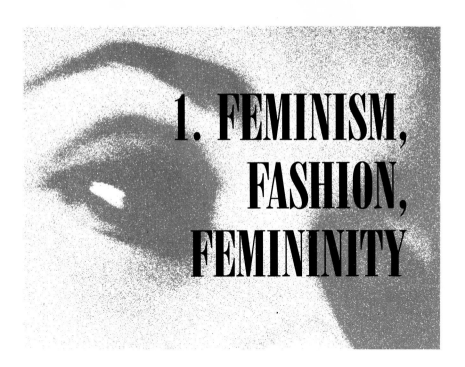

1. FEMINISM, FASHION, FEMININITY

BURNING FEMININITY: THE 1960s

The logic behind cosmetics is that the real you isn't enough. Feelings, dirt, hair must be controlled.

(Alice Embree, 'A Parable', Morgan, 1970, p. 212)

In the early years of the Women's Liberation Movement, the entire package of fashion was condemned by feminists. Liberation meant breaking out of the straitjacket of a controlled femininity. Dress, fashion and cosmetics were considered to be trivialities which functioned ideologically to construct a false femininity. Femininity was something that women had been forced to apply, to dress up in; liberation and the search for an authentic self meant taking it off, getting out of it. Beyond the joyfulness of the gesture, especially when made *en masse*, lay a complex of contradictions that were unresolved: what did it mean to get out of femininity?

The Women's Liberation Movement's categorical rejection of fashion was set against a specific background. The 1960s was a particularly fashion-conscious decade, one in which women ran the gamut of *personae* from spaced-out nymphet to earth mother. It was easy to get your wires crossed . . . If ideology can be understood as a practice of representations, 1960s' fashion took to heart its role of representing the feminine in a series of rapid definitions and redefinitions. Fashion was marked by its emphasis on youth. In 1960, David Bailey's photographs of Jean

Shrimpton defined 'the look' as girlish, helpless and scatty; a lack of equilibrium and control was eroticized. The irresistibly lost girl was epitomized by Edie Sedgwick, Warhol's 'favourite 60s girl' (Warhol, 1976, Chapter 2). In Britain Ossie Clark designed for a sort of pre-pubescent Alice. The attractiveness of the waif-like immature female body was an expression of fashionable deviance.

The mini-skirt was a little girl's garment and looked best on women like Twiggy who were built like little girls. Twentieth-century fashion has typically defined itself against the maternal body; early 1960s' fashion was hysterical in this respect. The attraction for women of fashions that embody the denial of the maternal is worth closer analysis. It has been proposed that the popularity of tight lacing among women in the nineteenth century is attributable to its anti-maternal significance in an age that prescribed maternity. Controversially, the corset might then be understood as a liberation garment, signifying a self-determined sexuality, distinct from the demands of procreation.[1]

The mini-skirt, as impractical in its way as tight lacing, was also anti-maternal. Combined with the 1960s' mania for thinness it expressed a resistance to the demands of mature femininity. Perhaps it is significant that the mini-skirt coincided with the introduction of the pill. Meanwhile, Pop Art celebrated the (plastic) inauthenticity of mass consumer culture, and its counterpart in women's fashion was found in a sophisticated pose of doll-like infantilism. This infantilism itself was complicated by the PVC and metal accoutrements of futuristic styles, as the mini-skirt stretched to take on its Action Girl connotations – from School Child to Space Cadet in one stride of your Courrèges boot.

In the late 1960s, 'the look' was increasingly formed by countercultural style that defined itself against the fashion establishment. Fashion came under attack, particularly from the hippy, student and youth movements. Hippy clothes expressed individualism, non-conformism, and a desire to be exempt from the dictates of Western consumer culture. On the left, the 'revolution duffle' condemned the élitism of fashion. All these movements were not bereft of their own subcultural style. But although they questioned the position of the individual in a mass consumer culture, women were still constructed as objects, even within the counterculture.

In terms of their sexual identity, women intercepted a deluge of contradictory demands at this period. Women's identity was defined, or positioned, by their appearance, an appearance of femininity that may have been particularly schizophrenic in the 1960s. It is interesting to speculate on this period as one in which the system that functions to control and define the feminine was overloaded. Perhaps the structure of systematic differences (for example, the virgin/whore dichotomy) breaks under the weight of too much contradiction. The result was the tearing of that particular veil: ideology was revealed as ideology. This overloading had its direct manifestation in fashion. The demand that one be a space-age, emaciated, neurotically sexual little girl was closely followed by the demand to be a hippy chick cum earth mother, the demand to be fake followed by the demand to be natural. These demands, and the insistence that in neither case must the labour show, let alone any sense of contradiction, are likely to put too much wear and tear on the ideology that holds femininity together.

The Women's Liberation Movement rejected fashion with anger, an anger that was informed by its recognition of fashion as an essential articulation of the ideology of femininity, a manipulative discourse about what women are, should be, or might become. In the 1960s the discourse of sexual liberation which the establishment called permissiveness and the counterculture called free love, paradoxically proved to be a controlling one for women. It was against the discovery of *false* freedom that the anger of the Women's Liberation Movement in 1968 shaped itself.[2] Left and right, counterculture and establishment, had something in common: both defined women in relation to their sexuality in such a way that appearance was still the dominant term.

In the unfocused anger of the feminist rejection of fashion lay a recognition that women's oppression had to do with the stereotyped idea of the female body as a sexual object. The first mass Women's Liberation Movement demonstration took place in Atlantic City in 1968 to protest against the Miss America beauty contest (Plate 1). Women felt manipulated by the demands of femininity, demands that always imposed themselves on the body. American feminists in particular identified a culture at war with women's bodies, constantly seeking to sanitize and deodorize, depilate, stereotype and control the unpredictable female body. In the discourse of the Women's Liberation Movement the emphasis on conventional femininity (and fashion) as a means of control was paramount. The initial aim was to 'get out' of fashion, however Utopian a project that may seem now.

In her anthology of writings from the early years of the Women's Liberation Movement *Sisterhood is Powerful*, Robin Morgan includes situationist-style essays on 'media images' that evoke that period of heroic feminism in all its impatience, insight and humour:

Hairsprays are the 'special forces' for dealing with the problem of hair-do sabotage. The threat of overthrowing the hair-do structure comes from the alliance between nature as an external liberating force and the natural movement of the hair itself. For this reason advertising lauds the merits of a hairspray by juxtaposing its capacity to hold a hair-do in place against the disintegrating powers of rain and wind.

Hairspray also acts as an invisible screen to prevent humidity from infiltrating and subverting an orderly coif into an unruly jungle.

Hairsprays are experts at 'holding power'. The labels advise women on the degree of control she thinks she needs: 'light' for the swinging natural look, 'regular' for those who want to be sure, and 'extra' for frizzy, unmanageable, fly-away hair.

(Florika, Morgan, 1970, p. 215)

The spirit and vocabulary of this text is borrowed from the language of contemporary liberation struggles, specifically the United States' war in Vietnam. Another extract makes references to the chemical war on women:

The warlike effort unleashed in the name of consumption has produced a strange imagery — especially for women . . . Ice Blue Secret is for 'a woman's extra feelings', but it is so those extra feelings won't betray her with their stickiness. The logic behind the commercial is that the extra feelings weren't legitimate; if they were, you wouldn't have to fear betrayal. The logic behind cosmetics is that the real you isn't enough. Feelings, dirt, hair must be controlled. The underlying message is one of self-control ('preventive warfare').

(Alice Embree, 'A Parable', Morgan, 1970, p. 212)

At the early Women's Liberation Movement demonstrations bras were rumoured to have been burned as a symbolic gesture. This legendary act immediately became a cliché by which a hostile press ridiculed feminism, and soon acquired mythic status. The furore it caused is more significant than whether bras were actually burned: as a clothing signifier in the hands of the Women's Liberation Movement the bra stood for the yoke of oppressive femininity; in the hands of the popular press the gesture represented the craziness of 'women's libbers'. Clearly they had touched a chord.

1. Picketing and guerrilla theatre during the Miss America Contest in Atlantic City, USA, 1968: the first mass demonstration by the Women's Liberation Movement. Photograph by Beverly Grant/ Newsreel

As a vestigial corset the bra stood for the whole history of women's oppression. If dress brings the body into culture, then underwear does so in a particularly intimate way. For the Women's Liberation Movement in the 1960s fashion's mediation between the female body and culture was seen as a form of control which was imposed from the outside, as Simone de Beauvoir had pointed out in the 1940s: 'Precisely because the concept of femininity is shaped by custom and fashion it is imposed on each woman from without' (de Beauvoir, 1972, p. 692). The bra covers the breasts and at the same time draws attention to them. It stands for the ritualized hypocrisy that feminists recognized as permeating the codes of feminine appearance. As a structure the bra suggested the need to reshape the female body. Bras give definition, they 'lift and separate'. For women, the bra is associated with 'becoming' a woman, acceding to femininity. Furthermore, underwear is private. To attack it in public exemplified women's determination to break the rules about the designation of public and private. Women's private anxieties were becoming the basis for public solidarity: anxiety could be turned into anger. Wearing a bra was associated with conforming to stereotyped femininity; discarding it signalled an end to that conformity. As a garment associated intimately with the cultural definition of the female body it is not surprising to see feminism associated with 'burning it'. The struggle was one of women's right to define their bodies themselves.

The feminist rejection of fashion was articulated as a repudiation of sexual stereotypes; implicit in this articulation was a rejection of narcissism. Narcissism is traditionally a female prerogative, a characteristic imputed to women within patriarchy to confirm their inferiority. In the 1960s and 1970s, feminism adopted the stance on narcissism that had been expounded by Simone de Beauvoir in the 1940s. De Beauvoir makes her critique of female narcissism central to the analysis of the cultural construction of femininity: 'Formal attire . . . is feminine narcissism in concrete form; it is a uniform and an adornment; by means of it the woman who is deprived of *doing* anything feels that she expresses what she *is*' (de Beauvoir, 1972, p. 543).

In her analysis of how 'in woman . . . the image is identified with the ego' (ibid., p. 642) de Beauvoir considers the way in which each woman is condemned to narcissism by a culture that treats her as an object. By implication the preoccupation with dress and appearance is to be despised as a tool of oppression, and narcissism is construed as a trap which prevents women from emancipating themselves. The preoccupation with a self-reflexive identity precludes women's access to the male world of action, thought and doing. It confines them to an imaginary rather than a 'real' world.

Furthermore, narcissism involves women in a dangerous 'comedy'. For de Beauvoir and for early feminism the struggle was to be taken seriously, to avoid ridicule. In this context fashion had to be abandoned, at least in principle. Paradoxically de Beauvoir champions the cause of women while endorsing a contempt for 'femininity'. A telling aspect of her discussion of fashion in *The Second Sex* is her hatred of female narcissism. It suggests the area as one of unresolved conflict.[3] Similarly the early Women's Movement, in its sweeping rejection of fashion, left narcissism and its relation to the construction of femininity under-explored.

By the mid 1970s, feminist dress exemplified de Beauvoir's position, signalling both practicality and indifference. It was important to show the lack of labour involved in self-presentation. Looking casual meant being yourself. It did not matter that the individual might spend some time constructing the look. Women wore dungarees and jeans; hair might be long or short but it was never 'styled' in any way; adornment was avoided — except in the form of badges — as were high heels. The only accessories were large holdall bags. This was conference and demonstration dress. Because fashion and femininity had been identified as so much labour, there was a problem with being seen to have 'done' anything. The idea was to present oneself unadorned, without any artificial intervention. Feminist anti-dress became both an attack on the power of fashion to represent women, and a search for a more authentic self.

The equation of authenticity with naturalness, however, brought its own problems. Janet Radcliffe Edwards comments on the 'muddle' in the feminist rejection of fashion about 'the natural person being the real thing' (Edwards, 1980, quoted in Wilson, 1985, p. 234).[4] Between friends, the question of depilation raged. Whether to shave legs, remove underarm hair? What could be more of a capitulation to arbitrary male tastes? Bodily hair of any sort is associated with sexual power in Western iconography; its removal then amounted to submission. Somehow the problem had not been solved if you did not shave your legs but always wore trousers.

In about 1973 David Bowie and his followers presented a radical attack on the way in which dress encodes and prescribes gender. This challenge was the opposite of the feminist attack on dress; instead of embracing the natural it embraced masquerade and artifice. But both had in common a challenge to prescriptive dress codes; although they clearly came from different positions, the stratagem of semiotic subversion in the Bowie model could be used by women too. There was a distinction between jettisoning femininity and actually dressing like a man. At this stage, the active desire to confuse became a way in which feminists positively began to negotiate style.

In the early 1970s perhaps the most conscious style that many feminists engaged in was Oxfam-shop and jumble-sale dressing, or retro chic. It had the merit of being cheap (maintaining a distance from the dictates of consumerism); in addition, it could keep its distance from fashion's denial of contrivance by being so obviously like dressing up in costume. Kaja Silverman suggests that retro chic 'puts quotation marks around the garment it revitalizes', allowing them to be re-read in the space of an 'ironic distance' between the wearer and the garment (Silverman, 1986, p. 150). Retro chic took as its models history and the cinema rather than *couture* and the catwalk. This allowed women the pleasure of dressing up without being positioned by fashion. A 1950s' lamé evening dress may quote Hollywood on female self-display while allowing the wearer to remain detached from that effect. Such a device gives the wearer the time and space to determine how she will present herself to the world, and allows a sophisticated fusion of ambiguity and irony.

REPRESENTATION: THE 1970s

The feminist rejection of fashion remained uncontested within the Women's Movement throughout the first half of the 1970s. Perhaps the intervention of punk in 1976 did more than anything else to re-open in the late 1970s the 'stifled debate' (Wilson, 1985, p. 235) about fashion and dress within feminism. In the late 1960s the Women's Liberation Movement had attacked the ideology of femininity head on. In the 1970s feminism focused on the question of representations of women, targeting in particular the cinema, advertising and pornography. These areas of enquiry gave rise to important contributions to feminist theory but the various debates rarely dealt overtly with fashion. For example, Helmut Newton's fashion images might be discussed but only to illustrate how pornographic codes permeated the media.

However, the conceptual vocabulary of the feminist critiques of representation may usefully be applied to the analysis of fashion. Fashion generates images that specifically address women. It is also possible to see dress and fashion as a way in which the body is 'pictured', by both wearer and spectator. Fashion is the discourse *par excellence* which articulates the theme of women's relationship to images of themselves. 'Women watch themselves being looked at' (Berger, 1972, p. 47). This characterization is an ancient one with an elaborate iconography. John Berger discusses how the iconography of fine art (painting) was extended to the representation of women in advertising and the media. His arguments helped to politicize the issue of representation and formed part of a wider response to the recognition that contemporary culture was increasingly dominated by images, and by images of women:

> . . . *men act* and women appear. Men look at women. Women watch themselves being looked at. This determines not only most relations between men and women but also the relation of women to themselves. The surveyor of women in herself is male: the surveyed female. Thus she turns herself into an object – and most particularly an object of vision: a sight.

(Berger, 1972, p. 47)

In the 1970s the feminist rejection of fashion was also a rejection of a system of representations, in which 'woman' is turned into a spectacle. Within that rejection was the recognition that fashion is more than handbags and skirt lengths; it is a discourse which constructs the feminine. It is easier, however, to jettison skirts and handbags than it is to get out of a system of representations. Fashion's representations were directed at women only. It was for this reason that fashion was largely ignored in the feminist attack on popular culture's images of women, which focused on advertising, pornography and mainstream cinema. The area of prime concern was the patriarchal fabrication and consumption of images of women. Women felt oppressed by the way in which they were represented and at the same time felt excluded from those representations; they felt both too close to these images and alienated from them. Where were pictures of women's labour, of old age, of motherhood, of female anger? There was no lack of imagery of the female libido but none, it seemed, determined by women. The power to represent was in male hands. Most importantly, the power to represent was just that – power – and women were excluded from it. Women were 'the defined sex' (Coward, 1984, p. 30) and they did not have a hand in those definitions. The power of representation was one of definition and it was primarily women's sexuality that was the object of that definition.

In 'Visual Pleasure and Narrative Cinema', Laura Mulvey took the discussion of women and the structure of representation several steps further (Mulvey, 1975, p. 6). The essay deals with mainstream Hollywood cinema and uses psychoanalytic theory to discuss the mechanisms of the spectator's pleasure in relation to the image. Mulvey discusses the image of the woman in narrative cinema as an erotic spectacle: 'Going far beyond a woman's to-be-looked-at-ness, cinema builds the way she is to be looked at into the spectacle itself' (ibid., p. 17). Within the representations of mainstream narrative cinema a woman is displayed as the object of a gaze that is both that of the male hero and that of the spectator in the auditorium. The central male figure in the film is active, he makes things happen. The spectator identifies narcissistically with the hero, the active male gaze within the film, and through him voyeuristically possesses the woman as spectacle within the narrative structures of the film. Thus: 'cinematic codes create a gaze, a world and an object, thereby producing an illusion cut to the measure of desire' (Mulvey, 1975, p. 17). She posits that 'in a world ordered by sexual imbalance, pleasure in looking has been split between active/male and passive/female' (ibid., p. 11). If looking is always active, and therefore always masculine, how then do women look? How is their visual pleasure catered for by cinematic codes or by other systems of representation? In a later essay Mulvey explored the idea of the woman spectator's identification with the masculine, active gaze, suggesting that women are in the habit of operating a kind of visual transvestism (Mulvey, 1981).

But fashion, unlike cinema, generates images of women for women, a system of representations that one might suppose to be cut to the measure of a *female* desire. Might there be a specifically female gaze and, if so, how would it differ from the masculine gaze? Could it involve narcissistic identification, a desire to look which is reflexive, constructing identity through likeness and recognition? Or is it with voyeuristic pleasure that women consume fashion images of women? Can the fashion image be read as an index of women's visual pleasure as it negotiates, appropriates, encroaches on, and steals the gaze within a patriarchal symbolic order? What are women doing when they look, look for pleasure?

At the end of the 1970s some feminist analyses of the ideology of representation focused with a special urgency on pornography, which was sometimes used as a point of comparison with fashion. If fashion is a text in which female desire is articulated, does that mean that the fashion image is merely an unacknowledged form of pornography for women? Does it make any difference that the representations of women in pornography conventionally address men while those of fashion address women? This point was usually ignored although the late 1970s and early 1980s saw the beginnings of a discussion within women's writing specifically about fashion imagery.[5] The debate on pornography touched on the nexus of image, power and pleasure, and discussed how pornography positioned women within the context of violence and masculine desire.[6]

Questions were asked as to whether one could make images of women *at all*, so paramount was women's objectification within all systems of representation. Kathy Myers referred to this impasse when she argued that the feminist critique of representation had come dangerously close to assuming that it was representation itself which degraded women. Such a position denies women the right to represent their own sexuality and 'sidesteps the issue of female sexual pleasure'. In an article in 1982 she argued that:

We have to understand the ways in which images work to construct our own experience of our sexuality. Rather than running away from the powers of the imagination and fantasy, we have to reappraise the role of representations in structuring our needs and desires as a step towards constructing new meanings for the experience and representation of our own sexuality.

(Myers, 1982b, p. 18)

She makes a comparison between the pornographic image and the fashion image, in this case a fashion advertisement for a bikini, and argues that 'selling female sexuality to a woman is not the same as selling it to a man' (ibid., p. 18). The pornographic image is structured to emphasize the accessibility of the model while the fashion advertisement trades on the proud aloofness of the model. Myers suggests that the fashion representation indicates a sexual power rather than sexual availability, or vulnerability.

Her article marked a turning point in the discussion of fashion in relation to feminism. Fashion, conventionally associated with female pleasure, became drawn into the feminist discussion of female sexuality. Specifically, the way was open for a deeper enquiry into fashion as a text in which, as Berger wrote, women 'watch themselves being looked at'. If this is so, how is the fashion image implicated in that process of self-objectification? The analysis of women's relation to the fashion image would contribute towards an understanding of the pleasure and pains of wearing fashion, a practice that is also largely about picturing oneself.

WHAT IS FEMININITY?: THE 1980s

The masquerade is a representation of femininity but then femininity is representation, the representation of the woman.

(Heath, 1986, p. 53)

The Women's Liberation Movement, in consciousness-raising groups and elsewhere, spoke of women's alienation from femininity: women produced it but they did not own it, they had to 'buy' it, actually and metaphorically. Femininity was something women were forced to inhabit and consume. When feminism rejected femininity it also rejected fashion as intrinsic to the construction, the lie, of femininity. Looking for an expression of an authentic 'natural' self, however, women based their appearance on a masculine model (short hair, trousers, no make-up) or an infantile model (coloured dungarees and lace-up shoes). The appearance of femininity was seen as some kind of contrivance but the validity of a masculine model went unquestioned. Currently women are using psychoanalytical theory to consider what value can be recouped for, or ascribed to, femininity itself.

Feminist debate has used psychoanalytic theory in developing a reading of how the construction of sexual difference positions the feminine as 'outside' or marginal to a culture whose order and language are patriarchal. This has generated a discussion of femininity not as conformism but as 'otherness'. Femininity was condemned as a lie by feminism but increasingly a circle has been drawn whereby women renegotiate a 'truth' about being female that exists within that lie.

In *The Second Sex*, de Beauvoir wrote 'One is not born, but rather becomes, a woman' (de Beauvoir, 1972, p. 295). She described the contradictions of femininity which she defined as being imposed and shaped from the outside, 'by custom and fashion'. Psychoanalytic theory, however, gives an account of human sexuality and the unconscious which investigates the way in which we internalize the social world in the process of becoming a woman or a man. Using this account, current theory on the construction of sexual difference posits a dominant patriarchy in which masculinity is the norm, femininity a *difference from*.

12

Further, psychoanalysis suggests that the construction of a gendered identity is precarious. This lends added weight to women's sense of alienation from femininity as a 'fixed' identity set up as the 'other' of masculinity. Women's resistance to femininity may be read not as an indication of the greater adequacy of masculinity but as a resistance to the way in which sexual difference positions and defines women. Seen as a discourse about femininity in its cultural construction, fashion may be read as a text not simply of a finished femininity but of the formation of that femininity. Fashion is the guided tour of feminine 'difference'.

If the cultural construction of femininity requires the definition of women's 'difference', fashion is a discourse that endlessly defines and redefines femininity. Indeed, it would seem that this practice of definition is central to the construction of sexuality itself: 'Women's bodies and the messages which clothes can add, are the repositories of the social definitions of sexuality. Men are neutral. Women are always the defined sex and the gyrations around women's clothing are part of a constant pressure towards the display of those definitions' (Coward, 1984, p. 30). Women must 'perform' femininity, and fashion is part of that performance. But femininity may be performed in different ways: contradiction may be articulated or denied.

Within the cultural construction of sexual difference women are identified with nature and men with culture. At the same time, women are required to exemplify artificiality while men are identified with authenticity. The opposition of nature and culture imposes on women an unresolvable cultural demand which is both moral and aesthetic. In attempting to replace artifice with authenticity, the Women's Movement had come up sharply against the many layers of contradiction which work to position women within the nature/culture split. 'Naturalness' was supposedly valued, yet bralessness, hairy legs and no make-up constituted a threat. The 'natural look' in fashion was not natural at all, it took as much labour as all the other 'looks'; its 'naturalness' was a function of the denial and concealment of that labour.

For women, fashion is both prescribed and reviled. It is prescribed as the aesthetic packaging of the female body; it is reviled as deliberate disguise and deception. Dress brings the body into discourse, mediating between nature and culture. As artifice, fashion transforms the 'raw' of woman into the 'cooked' of femininity; it produces the feminine within an opposition between naturalness and artificiality.[7] There is a morality attached to this opposition: adornment for the sake of conforming modesty is good, 'natural', while adornment for the sake of decoration is bad, wanton, immodest and artificial. Feminine adornment (or anti-adornment) is condemned or praised in accordance with whether the prevailing ideology of 'naturalness' has been disturbed or confirmed. That ideology, of course, is in a constant state of flux.[8] Cosmetics, the most quoted signifier of the wantonly artificial woman, may yet be used to signify modesty: 'in the 50s good girls wore lipstick'.[9]

The feminine, whether artificial or 'natural' is constructed through a system of adornment. Either way, the female body must not escape the controlling discourse of patriarchal culture: 'If . . . woman evades the rules of society, she returns to Nature and to the demon, she looses uncontrollable and evil forces in the collective midst' (de Beauvoir, 1972, p. 222). Fashion, by mediating the actual physicality of the female body, can order it and keep it at a distance.

If it is fashion that sets out the terms of this control, then fashion may also be used to subvert it. This is not done by attempting to resolve the impossibly contradictory position of women within the nature/culture split; but it may be possible to move into and inhabit that contradiction knowingly – to manipulate it, rather than be manipulated by it. The alienation that is a structural condition of being a woman forms a space which may be used strategically. Punk women were both highly confected and yet outside cultural norms. If fashion is one of the many costumes of the masquerade of femininity, then those costumes can be worn on the street as semiotic battledress.

In the late 1960s the feminist attack on fashion threatened the ideology of the natural. Women refused *en masse* to perform the ideological balancing act of femininity, poised between nature and culture. They fell from grace and were duly seen, in de Beauvoir's phrase, 'to return to Nature and to the demon'. Yet feminism has become trapped by that same ideology if feminists insist that the artificial, fashion, is 'bad', and posit an oversimplified concept of an authentic self, refusing to acknowledge the complexity of appearances.

The current feminist enquiry into the construction of femininity focuses on the alienation that is a structural condition of being female. This has furnished new ground for an understanding of fashion. Psychoanalytic theory has produced an understanding of the precariousness of female sexual and social identity, and invited feminists to re-evaluate the subject of female narcissism. Elizabeth Wilson discusses the ambivalence about fashion within feminism in *Adorned in Dreams*. She suggests, however, that ambivalence is ultimately an appropriate response to fashion:

This ambivalence is that of contradictory and irreconcilable desires . . . Fashion –

14

a performance art – acts as a vehicle for this ambivalence; the daring of fashion speaks dread as well as desire; the shell of chic, the aura of glamour, always hides a wound.

(Wilson, 1985, p. 246)

Fashion can be an experiment with appearances, an experiment that challenges cultural meanings. When women identify with fashion, they are celebrating experimentation. The feminist rejection of fashion was itself an experiment and it is now possible to imagine ways to direct that experiment back into fashion.

FOOTNOTES

1. See Kunzle (1982) and, for a response, Steele (1985). Many contemporary sources indicate that male opinion, medical and otherwise, was often eloquent in its condemnation of the practice.

2. For a history of the emergence of the Women's Liberation Movement in 1968 see Mitchell (1971).

3. It is partly this indication of conflict that saves de Beauvoir's thinking from simple puritanism. See also her brilliant and benign essay, *Brigitte Bardot and the Lolita Syndrome* (de Beauvoir, 1960).

4. Elizabeth Wilson writes of the 'stifled debate' about dress within feminism (Wilson, 1985, p. 235). She distinguishes two divergent ways of understanding contemporary culture that are reflected by a division within feminist thinking. She calls these divisions respectively 'authentic' and 'modernist', a division between 'on the one hand, those committed to "cultures of identity" and the achievement of true self and expression. On the other hand, those who act on the basis that human interaction depends on dissimulation, who insist on the central value of the city, its unpredictability, the fluidity of its codes and the subversive play with them' (Martin Chalmers, 'Politics of Crisis', *City Limits*, 19–25 August 1983, quoted Wilson, 1985, p. 231). Her book is a defence of the latter position and of fashion's importance in it. She suggests that an unresolved tension between the two positions 'haunts contemporary feminism' and has produced a feminist ambivalence about dress. 'Is fashionable dress part of the oppression of women, or is it a form of adult play? Is it part of the empty consumerism, or is it a site of struggle symbolized in dress codes? Does it muffle the self or create it?' (Wilson, 1985, p. 231).

5. See 'The Wound in the Face' (Carter, 1982), 'Fashion: Double-Page Spread' (Brooks, 1980), 'Signs and Whispers in Bloomingdales' (Brooks, 1981) and 'Fashion 'n' Passion' (Myers, 1982a).

6. See *Screen's* coverage of this debate from 1979 onwards.

7. For a discussion of how nature is 'cooked' in a consumer society see Williamson (1978), Chapters 4 and 5.

8. See Murray Wax, 'Theories in Cosmetics and Grooming', in Roach & Eichner (eds), 1965.

9. Angela Carter discusses the subversion of that signification, not by a 'natural' face but by wearing black on the lips, red on the eyes (Carter, 1982).

2. WOMEN AND PUNK: A CASE HISTORY

WOMEN, SUBCULTURE AND THE STREET

With punk, women were able to negotiate a social and ideological space for themselves through the deployment of oppositional dress. Unlike their male counterparts, women in youth subcultures have to contend not only with the dominant culture, but also with the patriarchal structures that are almost invariably replicated within the subculture itself. To examine the place of women within spectacular urban subcultures it is necessary to consider the designation of social space as private and public, the house and the street. Women have traditionally been associated with the private sphere, and to call into question the opposition of private and public space has important implications for women.

The obvious site for the manifestations of spectacular urban subcultures is the street, yet women's presence there is circumscribed in ways that are specific to their sex.[1] The opposition between the virtuous woman in the family and the fallen woman on the streets, which were the significant terms of the nineteenth-century discourse about women, continues to be played out in twentieth-century culture as the distinction between the 'good girl' and the 'bad girl'.[2] Punk commandeered the 'bad girl' look, in a strategy that separated it as a stylistic signifier from its ultimate signified, prostitution. The street is a crucial term in the consideration of women and punk, precisely because of the social and moral conflicts associated with women's presence there. It is central to the radicality of punk that in its initial moments in

17

1976 women were not marginalized within it as they had been in so many other youth cultures but were highly visible. This visibility was a function of the way in which punk style for women transgressed the strictures which govern women's presence on the street and intervened in the codes which determine women's appearance in relation to both class and sexuality.

Punk women both inhabited and turned on its head the contradiction whereby women are identified with nature as opposed to culture and yet are supposed to manufacture themselves as 'natural' beauties. They jettisoned conventional prettiness and sought instead to look tough, menacing and threatening. In doing so they pinpointed the masquerade of femininity, the unholy alliance of femininity, naturalness, good taste and good behaviour. In the mid 1970s feminist critiques of dress and fashion were still underwritten by concepts of authenticity and oppressive sexual stereotyping. To many feminists the paraphernalia of prostitution and sado-masochism was inevitably associated with the degradation of women. Yet, manipulated within the sophisticated subculture of punk, these accoutrements worked together effectively as a signifying practice, speaking the contradictions of femininity as vehemently and as articulately as feminist debate.[3]

The 'sexy' clothes of punk women made an intervention in the normal codes relating to women, appearance, class and sexuality. Punk was a grass-roots, aggressive, confrontational phenomenon which provides an ideal case history to demonstrate the use of dress and style in a strategy of resistance. By using the body itself as a site of signification punk women turned around the way in which the age-old identification of women with the body (as opposed to language and culture) serves to silence them.

Dick Hebdige has isolated two principal signifiers of punk: nihilism, or blankness, and sexual deviance, or kinkiness.[4] These two signifiers worked differently in the hands of either sex but were positively interpreted by both men and women. In part, it was in the play of one against the other that a space was made for the critical ambiguities of women's presentation of themselves. Hebdige writes of the importance of 'rupture' in punk discourse, the refusal to make meanings explicit or coherent. Punk's signifying practices 'gestured towards a "nowhere" and actively *sought* to remain silent, illegible' (Hebdige, 1979, p. 120). The cultivation of blankness contributed to an avowed repression of sexual difference: the sexual provocation of punk style was paralleled by an insistence on 'boredom'. The nihilistic anti-sexuality of punk was partly a way in which it differentiated itself from previous subcultures, particularly from the (ageing) hippy values of authenticity and love. It contributed to the intimidating alienness of punk, a feature shared by both men and women. For women, conventional ideas of prettiness were abandoned 'as though to be punk was to refuse to be intimidated into submissive femininity' (McRobbie, 1980). In terms of appearance the model was ostensibly a masculine one in that women sought to look menacing rather than pretty. The device of gender confusion inherited from glam rock and David Bowie was used for its power to make strange, to render alien. In punk the celebratory aspects of glam rock were overlaid with a nihilism even deeper than David Bowie's futuristic despair.

To some extent punk as a subculture reproduced patriarchal structures of male domination but its preservation of a nihilistic stance on sexuality, or on sex as simple pleasure, made possible certain sophistications in punk style for women. Outrageously 'sexy' clothes were worn as battledress in what Umberto Eco has called 'semiotic guerilla warfare' (quoted Hebdige, 1979, p. 105, and see Eco, 1986, p. 135). The nihilism and alienated sexuality of punk's stance attacked the tradition of romantic love, elaborated in magazines like *Jackie* and *My Guy*, which is such an important part of a girl's sentimental education. This attack on romance was perpetrated by the girls themselves rather than functioning to exclude them. Equally unusually in subculture, women had direct access to the darker romanticism of nihilism itself. The position of being outside normal cultural codes and practices contributed to an account of sex as hopeless, squalid and mechanical, an account which worked against popular expectations of youthful, especially feminine, attitudes.

The second of Hebdige's punk signifiers is that of sexual deviance. 'The paraphernalia of bondage – the belts, straps and chains – was exhumed from the boudoir, closet and porn film and placed on the street where they retained their forbidden connotations' (Hebdige, 1979, p. 108). When punk women appropriated the bad girl *look*, the separation of the look from its signified, sexual availability, constituted a form of deviance in itself. This was a refusal to submit to the pressure on women to be what they appeared. For women, the wanton use of the sexual codes of female dress is forbidden. While both sexes must submit to the pressure to declare themselves through dress – bankers must dress like bankers, secretaries like secretaries – there is an additional pressure on women to declare their relationship to men and to class through their appearance. A 'lady' is not just a middle-class woman, she is a chaste woman, or a married one. In the nineteenth-century city an enormous rise in prostitution co-existed with the middle-class cult of idealized femininity. While they shared actual physical territory, crossing paths constantly in the street, the 'fallen woman' and the 'perfect lady' occupied mutually exclusive ideological territory. As the environment of the industrialized city offered new possibilities of anonymity and adventure it was especially pressing for women to make their sexual identity clear. Such pressures have militated against women's use of the ambiguities that are operative in, for example, male dandyism, where an emphasis on appearance functions to withhold information as to occupation and identity. Punk's awesome manipulation of sexual clichés threatened the time-honoured codes that governed women's appearance on the street. The power of punk dress was the power to confound.

Punk fashion for women was an alternative to the perfect gloss of high fashion orthodoxy, with its notions of good taste, naturalness and wholesomeness, and its insistence on conventional beauty, slenderness and flawless skin. By contrast punk seized on the flashy, cheap and tacky: fluorescent colours, fake leopard-skin, fishnet stockings, plastic stilettos, pancake make-up and obviously dyed hair. These accoutrements together signified an interaction of sexuality and class that was resolutely unsoftened by tastefulness.

The traditional trappings of prostitution, signifying sexual availability, were combined with dress codes which drew more specifically on 'the illicit iconography of sexual fetishism' (Hebdige, 1979, p. 107–8) and generally on the iconography of pornography. While the paraphernalia of do-it-yourself hardcore fashion was common to both men and women it is not surprising that such a repertoire had a special significance for women. Within heterosexual pornography it is primarily the female body which is objectified and fetishized. In addition, there is a reticence about women as consumers of pornography, a reticence about where 'real' women stand in relation to its representations, which DIY hardcore fashion threatened, as it threatens all reticence about pornography.

Pornography exploits its own illicit status and punk flouted the stipulations as to its private and forbidden character. Punk women's use of pornographic signifiers was essentially ambiguous. In so far as punk clothes deployed the trappings of sado-masochism they were able to comment on the way sexuality is traversed by relations of power. Punk women paraded the streets wearing variations on pornographic images which were close enough to the original to be always unnerving. Punk mixed the more familiar clichés of the prostitute look with the strictly private, 'forbidden' gear of sado-masochism and fetishism. This was an offence against the distinctions and order of the representations of pornography.

Prostitution'

Pornography functions, among other things, to regulate and define sexual activity. Feminist critiques of pornography generally condemn the liberal view that the availability of pornography represents freedom of speech and understand both pornography and the state to be seeking to regulate female sexuality in ways that are not in the interests of women. Pornography intimidates women; porn shops are 'for men'. In terms of the deviance of punk style, women appropriated this forbidden discourse and redirected or undermined its meanings when, for example, they travelled on the tube covered from head to foot in black leather and chains. If women are 'the defined sex' (Coward, 1984, p. 30) then the scrambling of those definitions constitutes a critique of that system of definition. Punk style for women contained the seeds of the collective expression of a generation's maladjustment to femininity.

Against the background of early-1970s fashion, punk takes on new meanings. Punk's challenge to, and refusal of, high fashion was a way of targeting women's relation to the injunctions of high or mainstream fashion. Indeed after punk high fashion just lagged behind.

High fashion for women in the early 1970s was uncertain. Two looks predominated in the magazines: tweed (often in the ubiquitous hacking jacket) and the ethnic look. Yves Saint Laurent provided a *couture* version of the latter, plundering Russia, China and Eastern Europe for folk costume which the magazines presented in a format of wholesome glamour and sanitized luxury. (It is significant that when Vivienne Westwood looked to other cultures in the late 1970s she looked to traditional costume as it was still worn in Peru rather than to obsolete folk or peasant costume.) If there was a tension within high fashion it was no more than that between the sophisticated, international jet-set look, essentially urban and glamorous, and the more predominant pastoral, watered-down reworking of hippy clothes which emerged as either luxuriously ethnic or *faux*-naïvely milkmaidish.

The Japanese designer Kenzo represented the only critical development in high fashion for women during this period with quirky, off-beat and idiosyncratic designs which stepped beyond the parameters of the classy whore/tweedy lady dichotomy of most high fashion. With Jungle Jap, which opened in Paris in 1970, the ethnic look came of age. Kenzo juxtaposed fabrics and patterns with a wit that undermined the prevailing opposition between pastoral ethnicity and urban sophistication. He also withstood the hackneyed theme of the *femme fatale* in reworking children's clothes for women.

The context of 1970s rock music was crucial in the formation of punk style. From David Bowie and Lou Reed came a taste for androgyny and gender confusion.

The elaborate performances of Lindsay Kemp, and later the Rocky Horror Show, contributed, with varying degrees of relish or menace, to a kind of romantic and nostalgic decadence. Roxy Music's album covers exemplified a particularly early-1970s taste for highly styled pin-ups which became the hallmark of a new alliance between fashion and male rock culture. American bands like the New York Dolls, managed by Malcolm McLaren, and the Ramones were also influential. An especially important influence on punk rock style for women was the American rock poet Patti Smith, who repudiated femininity rather than blurring issues of gender in the way that Bowie did. She wore ties, waistcoats, braces and big jackets. In an interview she described how her sartorial models had always been men: Bob Dylan, Brian Jones, Jim Morrison, Jimi Hendrix and Rimbaud. The interview refers to her poem 'Female':

> Ever since I felt the need to choose, I'd choose male. I felt boy rhythms when I was in knee pants. So I stayed in pants. I sobbed when I had to use the public ladies' room. My under-garments made me blush. Every feminine gesture I affected from my mother humiliated me.

(*Honey*, February 1977)

Patti Smith's power as an artist denied this humiliation. Physically frail, her transvestite appropriation of heroic male gesture on stage, as she self-consciously mimicked Hendrix or Jagger, both acknowledged and denied the humiliations of femininity.

Subcultural styles were fragmented and diffused, unnoticed by the exponents of high fashion. Mainstream fashion was busy labouring over the old opposition between sexiness and class. When sex and class did interact in the discourse of fashion it was in ways which were defiantly reactionary, such as the photography of Helmut Newton or the underwear of Janet Reger. Angela Carter (1982) described the Janet Reger catalogue as an *objet de luxe*, an invitation to voluptuous or narcissistic fantasy, and the models in it as being also *objets de luxe*, as expensive to manufacture as the fragile ambiguities which adorn them.[5] Helmut Newton provided a more disturbing disquisition on the fashion model as object. His exploration of the connection between women's fashion and sado-masochistic fantasy was revealing if disquieting. A preoccupation with sexual decadence and pornographic imagery permeated fashion as it did all forms of popular culture. It took punk to know what to do with it.

SEX

In the 1970s Vivienne Westwood and Malcolm McLaren had a shop in the King's Road which was called consecutively Let It Rock (1971), Too Fast to Live, Too Young to Die (1972), Sex (1974) and Seditionaries (1977). Sex was the forum for the beginnings of punk. Westwood and McLaren produced the seminal bondage collection; it was for both men and women, and the predominantly black garments were studded, buckled, strapped, rubberized, slit and chained. The Sex Pistols, managed by McLaren, wore the collection on and off stage. The clothes had zips everywhere which made them gape in unusual places like the back of the legs. The collection was, according to Vivienne Westwood, carefully researched. In order to avoid any 'woolly' or 'liberal' gloss she worked with sado-masochistic 'equipment' in front of her, she talked to people who used it, and she incorporated its details into her repertoire, for example in bondage trousers, the legs of which were connected by a bondage strap.

> It's all a question of dynamics. The bondage clothes were ostensibly restrictive but when you put them on they gave you a feeling of freedom. They made you want to move your arms around. Clothes are about the body. To be sexy you don't have to have the two cheeks of your bottom clearly defined in a pair of denim jeans – that's not *necessarily* sexy. *Sex is fashion.* Fashion and sex are very intermingled; if you want to attract someone sexually, if you don't want to attract a chauvinist pig, then you've got to show you've got something going for you, if you're a woman, that you're in *control* of things – that's to do with sex.
>
> (Vivienne Westwood, quoted *ZG*, 1980, No. 2)

The dominant motifs clearly belonged to an occult field designated as sexual, but they were mixed with contrasting references. The whole shop at this time reproduced the intimidating secrecy of the 'exclusive' sex shop. The irony lay in its being a clothes shop, next to all the other boutiques in the King's Road, metaphorically beyond the pale in the aptly named World's End area. At one time the window was blanked out, with a small area of glass left that passers-by could peer through, as if through a key-hole, at a pornographic T-shirt, a leopard-skin stiletto shoe, or a piece of rubber wear. The shop sign – the word Sex – was in padded pink plastic letters but it was only *just* a joke. The particular mixture of blatancy and secretiveness was just idiosyncratic enough to mark it off from an ordinary sex shop.

Sex sold T-shirts bearing slogans with a range of sentiments calculated to disconcert, offend, or drive to apoplectic rage: Myra Hindley, Cambridge Rapist, Red Brigades and Paedophilia T-shirts, and others bearing slogans such as 'anarchy' and 'cash through chaos' (worn by the Sex Pistols) and 'destroy' (Plate 2). There were also Cambridge Rapist masks and pornographic T-shirts for which McLaren and Westwood were successfully prosecuted.

> With them [the pornographic T-shirts] you could find out where people's sore spots are and how free you really are. Sex is the thing that bugs English people more than anything else so that's where I attack . . .

(Westwood, quoted *ZG*, 1980, No. 2)

The two T-shirts seized by the police which resulted in Westwood and McLaren's prosecution were one depicting two cowboys with their penises hanging out of their trousers and one bearing the acronym 'scum'. During the trial it was explained to the bench that this stood for the Society for Cutting Up Men.

Plate 3 shows Siouxsie Sioux in a Sex T-shirt which has a photograph of a woman's breasts screenprinted on to it. Such clothes were demanding; for women the identification with pornography was particularly challenging. The clothes had to be worn with both aggression and irony, in the knowledge of what they signified.

One of the original and most visible exponents of the style was Jordan, personality, actress (notably in Derek Jarman's film *Jubilee*), and shop assistant at Sex. She wore the mixed uniforms of sexual fetishism, incorporating the occasional pastel-coloured twin-set, in a way that made her a public figure, incurring much the same opprobrium in the street that Quentin Crisp had in the 1940s. Ironically parodying the suburban housewife on a day-trip up to town she commuted daily from Brighton to London dressed in rubber and sharing a carriage with 'ordinary' commuters in pin-striped suits. It was a look city dwellers associate with private deviance but it was worn with an unexpected knowingness and defiance: the 'freak' turned cultural terrorist.

What women did with clothing in punk culture paralleled developments in punk music. The punk ethic that anyone could do it was exemplified by the fanzine Sniffin Glue's famous item, a diagram showing three finger positions on a guitar with the caption, 'Here's one chord, here's two more, Now form your own band' (quoted Hebdige, 1979, p. 112). Amateurism, anathema to fashion, was celebrated and

2. Vivienne Westwood in a Destroy T-shirt from Sex, 1976. Photograph by Norma Moriceau, courtesy of *i–D* magazine

became a key part of proto-punk style for women. Siouxsie Sioux made her debut by crossing the symbolic divide between audience and stage at a concert, starting as an 'ordinary' fan who just got up and did it. As all-women bands like the Raincoats and the Slits were formed, and performers like Siouxsie Sioux and Poly Styrene challenged every expectation about the conventional girl singer, women's position in rock music was radically changed. Women began to find their feet simultaneously in subcultural style and in rock music. Gradually a style developed among the all-women bands that was in many ways differentiated from the hard look of black-leather'n'chains classic punk. An unorthodox feminism produced a look that was both emphatically anti-bondage and in all its details disorderly, earthy and messy. The music they played was directly influenced by reggae and this allegiance corresponded to a style that was positively celebratory and carnivalistic. On stage and off the Slits put together anarchic and playful costumes of old clothes, little girls' dresses and tutus, worn with gum boots and dirty macs, dreadlocks and no make-up, or misapplied make-up. The distancing effect that punk women achieved through nihilistic styles was here replaced by a self-conscious infantilism in relation to clothes. Both forms of stylistic sabotage co-existed and interacted, allied in their attack on the codes of femininity.

SYMBOL INTO SIGN

In *Fashion and Anti-Fashion*, Ted Polhemus and Lynn Proctor define anti-fashion as fixed or slowly evolving clothing which upholds tradition and symbolizes the values of the social order it represents (Polhemus and Proctor, 1978). Folk costume and the Queen's coronation robes are examples of anti-fashion. Fashion is defined as a systematic, structured and rapid pattern of style change employed by the socially mobile, the rootless, and the alienated. Fashion tends to convert 'natural' anti-fashion symbols into arbitrary linguistic signs. Fashion acts to deprive anti-fashion images of their symbolic meanings so they become, like phonemes in verbal language, arbitrary building blocks in a new system of meaning.

In precisely this way, punk women took traditional anti-fashion symbols that were in themselves illicit and fashionalized them. The fashion parody of pornography and sex-shop dressing was central to the whole of punk fashion for women. These symbols of deviance were intended to deceive: punk women clearly

3. Siouxsie Sioux, of Siouxsie and the Banshees, on stage in a Sex T-shirt, 1976. Photograph by Sheila Rock

were not good girls, but it was not clear who was to profit (or indeed to suffer) from their badness. This was one of the most aggressive styles for women within any of the post-war youth cultures in Britain and represented a corresponding emancipation of subcultural style. Bondage dress allowed women to express the crudest will to sexual power or, indeed, to sexual victimization, while preserving a central ambiguity. As deployed on the street its ambiguity was, paradoxically, a function of its vulgarity: could a message so *blatant* be for real? Punk girls engaged *en masse* in the forbidden activity of confusing sexual messages; they looked like prostitutes but were something else. In fact this only became possible through the solidarity afforded by fashion, the safety of numbers (Plate 4). What had been achieved was the transposition of the garments from symbols into signs — a transposition which revealed the relations of power which operate to control the appearance of women.

Overall, punk women's clothing pointed to the interaction of sexuality and class, a combination always deemed particularly tasteless.[6] Alongside the explicit sexual iconography of the mini-skirts and suspenders, the cheap and trashy were celebrated: black roots on obviously peroxided hair, laddered and ripped stockings, PVC, lurex, fake leopard skin, kitsch designs in vulgar colours. Many of the things worn were not even items of clothing. Bin bags from the supermarket became dresses signifying both poverty and trash; razor blades, lavatory chains and tampons were similarly plundered from their normal contexts and, as items of adornment, were made to carry secret meanings which expressed resistance to the 'natural' order of the dominant culture (see Hebdige, ibid.). In addition, punk women were vehemently anti-naturalistic, in sharp distinction to the glowing good health of the Californian models on the fashion magazines of the 1970s. For women to choose so explicitly not to look natural was in itself an aggressive gesture. The punk *bricoleuse* went further still: she customized her own body. Hair stood on end in an unnaturally coloured tangle; make-up was worn not as an ingredient of 'prettiness' but to be seen as make-up, mask-like and tribal. Most of all, the safety pin lacerating the body came to stand in for violence. Often displaced from ear lobe to nostril or cheek, or multiplied up the side of the ear, it was awesomely permanent and effectively demarcated the weekender from the full-timer. Thus even the body, nature itself, was violated, transmogrified into a walking set of signs. The safety pin literally pinpointed this violation.

All this customization also spoke of visible labour: for the first time since the 1950s women were obviously 'got up', and their 'beauty secrets', or routines, were a mystery. There was a further irony in the way in which punk women took so

4. Four punk women in the King's Road, 1976. Photograph by Colin Jones

long to get ready and yet emerged looking, in the eyes of the dominant culture, threateningly hideous. The elaborate construction of the look also spoke an absence – absence of paid work, of cultural identity, of anything beyond the self as canvas. In this semiotic offensive the war was waged by women in the field of what Vivienne Westwood has called confrontation dressing.

The style of punk women was essentially ironic in its self-highlighting and self-referential blankness. Clearly women were not playing according to the rules: but what they were doing was less clear. Punk style was, as Hebdige has pointed out, intentional communication. It presented itself to be read and, perversely, misread. The syntax of its dress codes made no concessions. Punk women, by their juxtapositions and appropriations, did not so much resolve contradictions as raise them as issues. They were women but they appeared not to want to be 'feminine'; they were tarty but were not tarts; their appearance had a disquieting overtone of violence. In repudiating good taste, 'classiness' and naturalness they were a shock to fashion orthodoxy and to other women. As a method of dressing it was referential, tangential and encoded with meanings which were deliberately obscure, ironically juxtaposed, taken out of the closet and worn on the street.

If confrontation dressing had its pleasures they were enhanced by the more subjective pleasures afforded by the central ambiguities of punk style. For women there was excitement in exercising control over self-presentation, especially through the use of archetypally degrading garments, crossing an ironic or self-parodying feminine masochism with the delinquency of punk. Only when one has control over self-presentation can one enjoy the pleasures of dangerous imagery: the pleasures of control afford the pleasures of uncontrol. In the ironic parodying of the sex kitten, the predator, the vamp and the dominatrix, women could play with 'the disjunction between experience and signification upon which the whole style was ultimately based' (Hebdige, 1979, p. 122). This was an exercise of power, not in the literal sense, of what could be done, but on the level of representation, of what could be signified.

The ironic juxtapositions and the semantic instability of punk style worked together as the embodiment of contradiction. In the use of clothes charged with sexual meanings, a space was opened up for women to articulate and act out the contradictions and complexities within female desire, and within female desire as represented by men. The disjunction between what was worn and how it was worn expressed an ambivalence towards the sexual meanings of the clothes, clothes which were redolent of both victimization and erotic power. The dangers of such ambivalence for women were offset by the terms of punk irony, whereby the wearer herself 'put on' this display of contradiction. Such a display had all the satisfactions of a neurotic symptom which holds in suspension conflicting unconscious needs. Contradiction was embodied and articulated rather than resolved. Because the garments had ambivalent sexual meanings wearing them could express a conflict of desire. The pleasure was one of making neither affirmation nor denial, but of exhibiting a wound, 'a wound that is also a grotesque, capricious, barbaric adornment' (Paz, 1962, p. 17).

Punk women were threatening in the way that they appropriated a sexual iconography and subverted its meanings. Most importantly, they put this transgression on the street where it had the most impact. For women the trap of 'sexy' fashion is that its oppositional meanings are rapidly absorbed and converted; most damagingly, the vocabulary of sexual rebellion may be returned to that of sexual conformity. Eventually even the transgressions of punk style were legitimized or 'pardoned'. The punkette, cosmeticized and toned down, became a 'type'. By 1979 the National Westminster Bank was using black-leather-clad 'bad girls' in their advertisements. The 'bad girl' was taken off the streets and reinstated on billboards. As part of the advertising industry's iconography she was assigned a role in the economy. The punkette even reappeared as pornography's 'bad girl': the rupture was healed. When Zandra Rhodes produced her *couture* version of the style in 1979 – a meticulously torn, beaded, diamantéed, safety-pinned and zip-riddled black evening dress which is now in the Victoria and Albert Museum's costume collection – she healed one of punk's crucial dislocations as far as punk style for women was concerned: she applied taste to the wound and made it 'pleasing' (Plate 5).

Hebdige describes the process of incorporation whereby subculture's deviance is returned to the dominant culture through a process of media attention and explanation, and by the conversion of subcultural signs into mass-produced objects (Hebdige, 1979, pp. 92–9). All subcultures establish trends which feed back into the dominant culture and, in fashion as elsewhere, nonconformist space must be continually renegotiated. By a process of symbiosis subcultural 'deviance' is disarmed. The 'secret' objects of subcultural style are made available in high-street newsagents, record shops and boutiques. The oppositional meanings are compromised and qualified as the style is recycled by the dominant culture and put to different use. Punk rapidly altered from its first manifestations in 1976. It became polarized between its high fashion adherents and its tribal ones. In this latter form

5. Applying taste to the wound: Zandra Rhodes' *couture* version of punk, an evening dress of 1979 worn here by Debbie Harry of Blondie. The dress is in the Victoria and Albert Museum's collection. Photograph by Sheila Rock

punk continued, and continues, to exist as folk costume, just as Hell's Angels and Teds continue to exist. As folk costume the style is returned to anti-fashion, its 'forbidden' objects reconverted from sign into symbol. If the pre-1976 sado-masochistic gear was anti-fashion, it enjoyed only a brief period as 'fashion' before being returned to anti-fashion as a newly legitimized form of folk costume or tribal dress. A particularly 'gothic' version of punk persists as a tourist attraction in London's streets. Tourist shops sell postcards of punks next to those of the Royal Family. Although this case history is concluded with punk's absorption into high fashion, or conversion into folk culture, the story does not end there. Punk also set in motion, or made possible, most of the significant developments in fashion in the following ten years.

FOOTNOTES

1. For a discussion of these points see McRobbie (1980).
2. T.J. Clark, writing about women in the nineteenth-century city (in this case Paris), argues that: '. . . the prostitute was necessary to the articulation of discourse on woman in general. She was maintained – anxiously and insistently – as a *unity*, which existed as the end-stop to a series of differences which constituted the feminine. The great and absolute difference was that between *fille publique* and *femme honnête*: the two terms were defined by their relation to each other' (Clark, 1980, p. 23). McRobbie (1980) cites the bourgeois domestic values of the nineteenth century which functioned to regulate women's behaviour.
3. In 'The Expressive Style of a Motor-Bike Culture' (Benthall and Polhemus, 1975, p. 233), Paul Willis writes:

Whereas 'deprived' minority cultures do not use verbal codes to express their meaning, they do have complex feelings and responses which are expressed in their own culturally resonant way. Essentially these groups have forms of expression quite as rich and varied as those in apparently more 'accomplished' cultures, but in a mode which makes them opaque to verbally mediated enquiries and therefore vulnerable to gross minimization in conventional accounts . . . it is *because* these codes of expression are largely passed over, or misinterpreted, by the middle class and their agencies of control that they can, and are allowed to, play such a vital part in the generation of minority cultures with critical stances towards the dominant culture . . . certain styles and activities within a minority culture, far from being meaningless or random, may in fact perform something like the same expressive function that language does in the more familiar (to the middle classes) culture.

He goes on to suggest that (ibid., p. 251)

We must consider that the body (as opposed to the head, language) is used in certain minority cultures . . . to express coded, and partly hidden, opposition to dominant culture surrounding them – in a way that language, even where it could effectively be used, would never be allowed to.

4. We have drawn heavily on Hebdige (1979), which looks at punk and other post-war youth subcultures in terms of class and race but not gender.

5. Angela Carter writes: 'this is part of the "fantasy courtesan" syndrome of the sexy exec, a syndrome reflected admirably in the pages of *Cosmopolitan* magazine. Women regain the femininity they have lost behind the office desk by parading about like a *grande horizontale* from early Colette in the privacy of their flats, even if there is nobody there to see' (Carter, 1982, p. 97). The same idea was dealt with in psychoanalytic terms by Joan Rivière in *Womanliness as a Masquerade*, in which she described the processes of over-compensation whereby professional women put on 'a mask of womanliness' as a defence, 'to avert anxiety and the retribution feared from men' (Rivière, 1986, p. 35).

6. See T.J. Clark's discussion of the bourgeois outrage at Manet's *Olympia* in *The Painting of Modern Life* (Clark, 1985, Chapter 2).

3. BLITZ CULTURE: GENDER AND THE REINVENTION OF THE SELF

CROSS DRESSING

I wanted to reinvent myself.

(Annie Lennox, quoted *Guardian*, 26 November 1986)

A feature of London fashion during the late 1970s and early 1980s was the blurring of sexual divisions in an orgy of costume. Theatre has always extended the prevailing social limits of what can happen in dress: it is not 'real life'. The institution of transvestism in the theatre survives in the form of the pantomime dame and the principal boy. In the early 1980s the streets of certain sections of the city, the new clubs and the new magazines formed a stage on which dress and fashion could become costume. The barriers against transgression were all but pulled down in the transposition from real life to theatre. One of the chief weapons of punk style was the way in which it sustained uncertainty and doubt as to whether its pornographic and derelict poses were 'for real' or not. It questioned the very categories of authenticity and inauthenticity, reality and pretence. In Blitz culture's excesses that doubt was removed: this was theatre. The style was constructed by a manipulation of images, stereotypes and assumptions. In so far as it was men who were seen to be most dominant in their manipulation of gender, male sexual power was symbolically reasserted within subculture. Men could magically transcend both masculinity and femininity by juggling with the signifiers of gender. In cross dressing they had access to the semiotic possibilities of the control and manipulation of the signifiers of femininity. As masquerade, femininity was up for grabs.

'LOST BOYS': THE THEATRE OF ANDROGYNY

'In every human being a vacillation from one sex to the other takes place, and often it is only the clothes that keep the male or female likeness, while underneath the sex is the very opposite of what is above.'

(Virginia Woolf, 1942, p. 109)

Late in 1978 a new subculture began to emerge. It started in a club in Meard Street called Billy's run by Steve Strange and Rusty Egan, whose Bowie Night ran weekly for three months. In February 1979 it moved down the road and became Blitz, with Egan as DJ, Strange as greeter; its *habitués* were widely written about as Blitz Kids or New Romantics. They tended to be art students or unemployed. Many of them subsequently made a name for themselves as designers, film-makers or pop musicians. They included the designers Stephen Linard, David Holah and Melissa Kaplan, Boy George, Jeremy of Haysee Fantayzee, Spandau Ballet, Ultravox, the film-maker John Maybury, Binnie, performer, and Denzil, model and clubber. Blitz was a club and it had a door policy. People were vetted for entry solely according to their looks and their clothes. From the start it was a highly narcissistic cult; individualism was prized. Steve Strange was its publicist. *Blitz* magazine (not connected to the club) describes an odyssey which sent Strange across the pages of the magazines:

All by virtue of a carefully self-projected and manipulated *style* . . . what is the man's claim to fame? Quite simply, nothing. He has served as the most exquisite silent screen for the projection of sartorial elegance – fashion-marketing; night-clubbing; and most recently, musical dilletantism. Focal point of the self-styled 'cult with no name', our intrepid Peter Pan has conjured up a crèche of lost boys, not with an ideology, but rather the sole intention of entertaining themselves before any available audience.

(*Blitz*, Issue no. 2, Spring 1981)

36

'Lost boys' found themselves and their lost narcissism in the Never Never Land of the clubs. But what happened to the girls? To a great extent women lost what punk subculture had given them: street visibility. The radicality of punk fashion for women gave way to the radicality of the massing of boys as spectacle, the radicality of men moving in on the cultural space of femininity: excess, artifice, narcissism.

The New Romantics' aesthetic at the beginning of the decade was hedonistic, glamorous and luxurious, unlike the poverty-chic of punk. The emerging club scene spearheaded by Blitz co-existed symbiotically with a rash of new magazines which documented it: *Blitz, i-D, The Face*. Punk's DIY fanzines and its visible rupture with the past in terms of style may have been an inspiration or concrete example of how to do it. Steve Strange moved on to host the Club for Heroes (where in 1981, Westwood and McLaren showed their Pirate collection, with the slogan 'clothes for heroes') and then the Camden Palace. Countless other clubs sprang up – Gaz's Rocking Blues, The Fridge, Le Beat Route, The Dirt Box, The Batcave, The Gold Coast, The Wag, The Mud. Perhaps the last in this tradition was Taboo in 1985 hosted by Leigh Bowery. As the clubs proliferated in the early 1980s so did the styles. Blitz seemed to be a Pandora's box; it was followed by a hysterically speeded up turnover of looks: New Romantics, rockabillies, New Psychedelia, Regency fops, bobtails (artificial dreadlocks woven into hair and bound with rags), zoot suits, flat tops, African prints, 1960s pastiche (beehives and winklepickers). Kate Garner from Haysee Fantayzee wore Afro-Dickensian dreadlocks. Boy George rose to fame wearing Hassidic ringlets. Fashion itself became fashionable. There was a band called Fashion and a club called Total Fashion Victims. The phenomenon of extravagantly dressed and decorated men developed into a street style which was labelled 'peacock'.[1] The peacock male was a fop rather than a dandy in the sense that the dandy originally exemplified a restrained male elegance whereas the fop, an eighteenth-century phenomenon, was a figure identified with femininity and folly through excess in dress. Stephen Linard, New Romantic, Blitz *habitué* and fashion designer who graduated from St Martin's in 1981, was highly influential. For men he designed tailored clothes with shirts in organza, a fabric which is floating and see-through, previously associated with the sort of romantic evening gowns worn by Grace Kelly. John Crancher subsequently took this use of see-through fabric further. Since the Great Masculine Renunciation[2] of the nineteenth century, the use of sensuous fabrics in men's clothes had been associated with a rebellious stance. Oscar Wilde promoted the use of silk and velvet; in the 1960s men wore satin, floral prints and bright colours. Blitz style took these transgressions further.

In *Dressing Up: The History of an Obsession*, Peter Ackroyd distinguishes two types of transvestism: the fetishistic and the anarchic. Fetishistic cross-dressing is historically a later form, particularly reinforced in the nineteenth century when transvestism became more exclusively associated with sexual perversion and secrecy. In contrast, the anarchic form is celebratory and openly subverts the social order. Ackroyd discusses androgyny as the representation of an original state of power in many cultures, a symbolic transcendence of the binary opposition between male and female; transvestism combines and confuses the attributes of both sexes. The anarchic possibilities of cross-dressing were explored in the classical festivals such as Saturnalia. Medieval Christianity criticized the Feast of Fools in which both laymen and clergy dressed as women; in the sixteenth century the Feast of Fools was secularized in the festivities associated with the election of the Lord of Misrule in which women as well as men dressed as the opposite sex. Cross-dressing, an emblem of misrule, is 'pervaded by the notion of the ultimate triumph of Chaos' (ibid., p. 52).

Like carnival, the clubs of the early 1980s occurred regularly but not every day. They permitted contained (sartorial) unruliness, which was often not tolerated on the street where such costume would sometimes arouse verbal abuse or even physical violence. A plenitude of styles prevailed, excessive and heterogeneous. The social and sexual order was reversed and mocked (Plate 6). For a night men could be women, the unemployed could dress as kings and queens, as Hollywood stars, aristocratic Regency fops or ecclesiastics (there was a minor fashion for ecclesiastical dress which neatly inverted the medieval carnival custom of ecclesiastics dressing as laymen and women). Boy George wore a nun's habit (see *i-D*, 4, 1981, for a picture) among his many costumes; his relentless innovations resulted in a plethora of different personae (Plate 7). Later, the eighteenth-century look was taken over by very young aristocrats and débutantes (issues of *Harpers* and *Tatler* showed exhausted young people flopping on sofas in ball gowns), as if to confirm that there had been a real reversal when unemployed or working-class clubbers had dressed like viscounts at a ball.

Peter Ackroyd describes a tradition of male cross-dressing that started to go underground in the seventeenth century when men ceased to act women's parts on stage, and was totally submerged during the nineteenth. Blitz, and club culture generally, was not a 'coming out' of a hitherto furtive 'perversion'; it signified a return to the anarchic (public and joyful) rather than to the fetishistic (private and shameful).

6. Male masquerade: a hard act to follow. Man and woman at the Blitz club, 1980. Photograph by Ted Polhemus

In the twentieth century the power of transvestism to shock lies precisely in its association with private perversion. While Ackroyd's distinction between fetishistic and anarchic forms of transvestism is a useful one, it was the mixture of the fetishistic and the anarchic, the inability to separate them out, that characterized Blitz culture. 'Dressing up' (that is, as a woman) is perverse only for men. Boy George could insist that he was a boy, and just playing, but his insistence was only meaningful in the face of a lingering public scepticism. While punk took pleasure in manipulating that kind of public doubt, Blitz culture routinely disavowed the charge of deviance and gained its effects through an insistence that there was 'no difference' between trousers and skirts, men and women, sex and a cup of tea. (Boy George, in an interview in *Woman's Own*, when asked about his sexual preferences, replied, 'I'd rather have a cup of tea.') Blitz culture's transvestism signified a tribal refusal to recognize or acknowledge difference, in a kind of group narcissism.

Although punk insisted on meaninglessness and vacancy, in many ways that was a rhetorical device to give voice to the real poverty and deprivation of the dole queue. In the early 1980s unemployment continued to rise. Punk had posited 'no future' in 1977. In 1979 the New Romantics held a costume ball, its theme 'dress for the future'. They came largely not in recognizable futuristic outfits but in a series of styles plundered from the past, ranging from Regency fops to Elizabethan costume (Plate 8).

In another dramatic reversal, the future was a return to the past. Stephan Rainer, co-owner of **PX**, the shop where many of the New Romantics bought their clothes, said, 'We're a reaction to the microchip' (*Blitz*, 2, 1981). Vivienne Westwood and Malcolm McLaren's Pirate collection was highly influential but there was a subtle ideological difference between the New Romantics' nostalgic recreation of the past on the one hand and the subsequent postmodern creations of McLaren and Westwood on the other. Westwood went on to use stockinette (a fabric for cleaning cars) in her toga dress, the New York graffiti artist Keith Haring's prints in the 1984 Witches collection, and Third World influences in her Buffalo Girls collection. In music, McLaren discovered hip-hop, scratching and musical *bricolage* (in his records *Duck Rock* and *Madame Butterfly*). McLaren, like Warhol before him, found a way to make a series of critiques of consumer culture through embracing it, 'liking it' and exploiting it. The New Romantics' critique was more conventional; but it won them subcultural space, which is the first requirement of subcultural movements.

The New Romantics were defiantly apolitical. Carnival is not about being

7. The Scheherazade Look: Boy George in one of his many personae at the St Moritz club, 1980. Photograph by Ted Polhemus

progressive, rational or compassionate (all ideas of the Left): it is Dionysiac, not Apollonian. In a sense it is inappropriate to speak of the New Romantics as belonging to the Left or the Right. Implicitly they rejected feminism as part of a moralistic progressive package. Their exclusive door policies and the sense of a new aristocracy of dress display the élitism of the marginalized. Yet the New Romantic moment made a space for that which is not normally countenanced: excess, prodigality, heterogeneity, narcissism and, above all, the infantile, allowing access to the uncharted areas of the carnivalesque.

The 'peacock' style pioneered by men was a hard act for women to follow. It is interesting to compare how women dressed in the clubs to the early work of Cindy Sherman, a New York artist who photographed herself in a series of disguises in different locations for her *Untitled Film Stills*. The cumulative effect of looking at a lot of pictures from this period is very similar to the cumulative effect of looking at Sherman's work. In the clubs net, tulle, lamé, lace, tartan, *broderie anglaise*, fishnet, 1950s kitsch, corsets, ball gowns, swimming costumes, fur, make-up, endlessly grouped and regrouped in shifting combinations to form a composite image of femininity (Plates 9 and 10), an image which shifted between men and women with tremendous fluidity and ease. Like Cindy Sherman, women (and men) raided the image bank for signifiers of femininity, so that femininity itself came to be seen as an infinite number of appearances, divorced from biological sex.

Cindy Sherman makes a critique of femininity in her series of infinitely recurring variations on a theme. But in the clubs fashion offered women more than a shifting picture of themselves. Girls used the subcultural space of the clubs to have fun, especially through dressing up which might become less the means to pleasure than the end itself. Dressing up allows the possibility of narcissistic speculation, curiosity, dressing up together in pairs, comparing, contrasting and giggling, a possibility of fantasy and exploration, not in any sense of finding a 'true self' but, rather, of exploring the shifting relation between being and appearance, seeing and being seen. In the clubs women acted out the multiplicity of selves that Cindy Sherman's photographs present. In many ways, this is the traditional stuff of the feminine position: dressing up and going out. The club culture of the early 1980s offered only an extension of the conventional practice.

Femininity was analogous to a kind of masquerade, or performance. The clubs, crucially, blurred the boundary between performer and audience. A notable figure on the early club scene, and much written about, was the performance artist Binnie (Plate 11), who appeared naked, her breasts and belly bulging like an ancient

8. Man and woman in Elizabethan dress at the Blitz 'Dress for the Future' night, 1980. Photograph by Ted Polhemus

fertility symbol, her body smeared in paint, with matted, witch-like hair, strikingly distinct from the vertical or neatly coiled hair-dos around her. As the 'natural' woman she performed yet another act in the masquerade of femininity. Her nudity was a form of dress. On the other hand, hers was an act that men could not replicate.

CAMP FOLLOWERS

In the clubs of the early 1980s, femininity was increasingly colonized by men in their clothes and make-up. Men were the style leaders: Steve Strange, Stephen Linard, Stephen Jones, Philip Sallon and, later, Leigh Bowery. In the clubs men's cross-dressing sometimes reinforced a stereotype of femininity, rather than upsetting preconceptions about gender. Blitz culture looked like carnival, with all its role reversals, but sex is never a straight reversal. If part of the power of subculture is to frighten, to place oneself beyond the pale and to be a voluntary outcast, there was more scope for men in Blitz. There is less threat in women's cross-dressing; it is a sign of aspiration, moving *up* the patriarchal heirarchy. The powerful taboo is against male transvestism, partly because of entrenched homophobia, partly because it is a step *down* the social ladder. Through cross-dressing Blitz culture gave men access to dread, and to the power to frighten, which women wearing suits do not have.

Men's fashion became progressively more peacock-like as men escaped the straitjacket of conventional male dress, as if through transvestism and drag they found an expressive medium for their narcissism in a dominant culture which prohibits male narcissism in dress. Femininity thus became common currency in the clubs:

now it [unisex dressing] is back under a new heading. Now it's trans-sex, which is a million times more exciting. You've got this dull-looking girl standing next to this beautiful girl, which, when you look closely is, in fact, a boy who has put on women's clothes and sometimes looks better than a woman . . . We have this transexuality that is affected by this male idea of a woman, which is a domineering female. Whenever you look at a male fantasy of a woman, it is really a man with stuck on buttocks and tits . . . I'm certainly going to do female clothes in drag sizes from now on because they are much more exciting. I'm sick of dressing women who don't know whether they are trying to please men or other women.

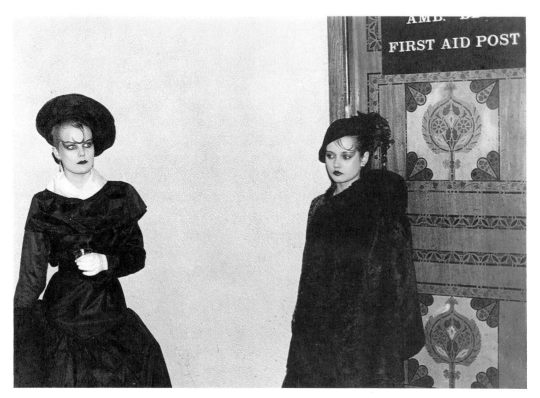

9. Two women in débutante mode, clubbing at the People's Palace, 1981. Photograph by Ted Polhemus

Men don't give a shit. All they want to do is please other men. Homosexual or straight, they still want the opinion of their mates . . . Women with bits of rags in their hair and wearing ra-ra skirts! It's just a long way from what I've been describing. The boys are nearer to it. They have wanted women to be like that for so long but women have not tuned into it. So they've ended up doing it themselves.

(Anthony Price, quoted Kytsis, 1983)

This statement, striking for its contempt and misogyny, endorses the theory of the patriarchy as being more or less a homosexual culture, in which men either give in to, or desperately protect themselves from, the possibility or threat of homosexuality. In this schema it is women's *difference*, their castration, which upsets men more than anything – so that, according to Anthony Price, men dress for men, and women fail to dress successfully for men.

Cross-dressing can subvert and undermine the hierarchies and structures of gender division. In the early 1970s David Bowie popularized androgyny and bisexuality; the style of his stage personae proposed a challenge to the categories of the masculine and the feminine by pointing to the cultural construction of gender. This bisexuality became a third term which allowed both men and women to scramble meanings about gender. The Bowie model opened up possibilities for women as well as men. 'I love the sound of the sax, but I think it was David Bowie's brown zoot suit and carroty hair – and sax – in his *Pin-up* days, that did it. I thought I could look as cool as that!' (Clare Hurst, quoted Steward and Garratt, 1984, p. 106).

But although Steve Strange claimed Bowie as an influence, the carnival which he set in motion seemed to offer less to women. The club 'hosts' created fantastical and quirky personae through dress. But when men turned to cross-dressing they tended to parody femininity. Generally, men's 'use' of femininity was exclusively theirs in that, as Anthony Price suggested, it was addressed to other men. It was unfashionable to be a woman, fashionable to be a man, and most fashionable to be a man dressed as a woman.

In these circumstances a woman who wanted to be fashionable could do one of three things. She could dress in outrageous corseted satin dresses and diamanté, just like the boys (Plate 12 – a bared breast goes one better, flaunting the one thing they haven't got). Secondly, she could dress like a party piece, drag-queeny but

10. Two women masquerading at the People's Palace, 1980. Photograph by Ted Polhemus

humorous, a kitsch object, like Mari Wilson with her Neasden beehive or Lena Lovitch who moved through Carmen Miranda and Miss Haversham to Mata Hari. It was as if women had to demonstrate, by wearing on their sleeve, and not only there, their capacity and willingness to be good sports, to make a 'guy' of themselves. They could be camp followers. The third option was to dress in versions of the new Japanese designers like Yohji Yamamoto and Comme des Garçons, in clothing that was dark, loose, androgynous and asexual – very much how men were dressing when they weren't being women. This side-stepped the question of gender altogether, as if its wearers got out of sexual difference by getting out of Western culture.

GENDER BENDING

Punk had ruptured the 'natural' connection between the way a person looked and their sexual proclivities, opening up the space for Blitz culture's transvestism. Gender and sexual preference were sundered; heterosexual men could dress as women and vice versa. Dress in Blitz culture was never a method for communicating a sexual choice. Pop musicians further widened the gap between what one looked like and what one wanted. Among women, Grace Jones was marketed as a camp dominatrix and Annie Lennox raided the image bank to resemble Bowie ten years earlier. She pioneered a hard-edged, glossy transvestism out of professional necessity.

> I wanted to look sharp but accessible. I needed to project my individuality and avoid being categorized as another 'little girl singer' – a suit and a tie were an important aspect of this. I don't mind if people misinterpret my appearance; I play games to protect myself.

(Annie Lennox, quoted *Vogue*, March 1984)

While Annie Lennox had more influence on fashion stylists, ironically, young girls chose to model themselves on Boy George. George's femininity was safer than Annie Lennox's repudiation of it. Clearly the sex underneath being 'the very opposite of what is above' (Woolf, ibid.) was no deterrent. The *Sun* coined the phrase 'gender bending' in 1983. The phenomenon, once named, became cosy and safe. Boy George played up to it: he claimed to prefer tea to sex, he was cuddly and loveable. Like a geisha girl for girls, meticulously confected and designed to please,

11. Playing nature to his culture: Binnie and an unidentified man at Hell, May 1980. Photograph by Ted Polhemus

Boy George presented them with a sexual identity that was under control because it was self-constructed, a femininity that was safe, yet both sophisticated and innocent.

> George, though he does his damnedest to look as glamorous as possible, has always maintained that he is only what he makes of himself, that anyone can make the effort. George speaks to all the fans who are overweight or troubled with acne or otherwise unconfident about their appearance. He tells them they needn't worry about it, that he doesn't care and offers them a glittering example of what can be done with some imaginative clothes and a generous dab of make-up . . . In genuinely discounting the importance of natural, as opposed to artfully constructed, beauty, George gave hope to thousands of potentially insecure teenagers.
>
> (Rimmer, 1985, p. 112)

GENDER JUGGLED

While George was fashionalizing femininity in 1983, *The Face* and *Blitz* started doing features on Bronx rappers, scratchers and break-dancers. Malcolm McLaren's *Buffalo Gals* video (January 1983) sparked off a break-dancing craze. Malcolm McLaren was quoted as saying: 'The best ideas come from the gutter' (*Blitz*, 16, November 1983); the concept of 'street' came to connote integrity, authenticity and toughness. *The Face* did articles on break-dancing, rapping and hip-hop; at the same time it introduced fashion spreads for men which were clearly homo-erotic, putting boxing and cycling gear on very pretty, beef-cakey boys. The homo-erotic possibilities of this look were furthered by the British fashion for black American ghetto music, culture and style, a fashion which emphasized the male orientation of the style and ignored women rappers for some time. January 1984 saw the first cover boy on *The Face*, which had always featured male pop musicians but not male models, and the magazine continued the trend throughout 1984. Increasingly men replaced women on the fashion pages as figures for narcissistic identification and contemplation. In September *The Face* set in motion the final stage of the Great Feminine Renunciation.[3] It was a combined fashion spread which showed men's bodies cut up and segmented, nose to knee, with a pastiche of a *Cosmo* quiz on sex which was, however, addressed to men, not women:

12. The genuine article: clubber at Blitz, 1980.
Photograph by Ted Polhemus

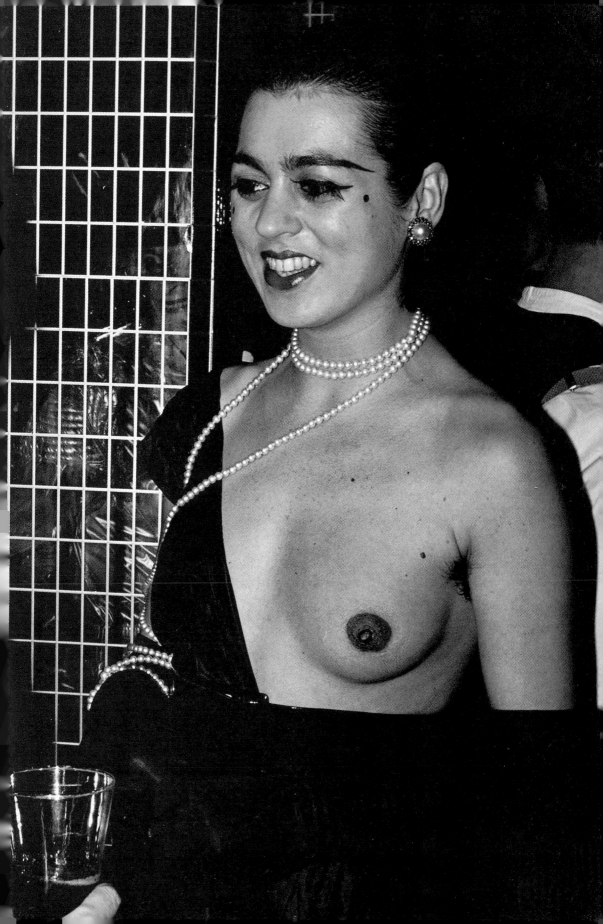

1. YOU HAVEN'T PULLED FOR WEEKS. YOU BLAME . . .

    a) Your body

    b) Your make-up

    c) Oppressive sexual stereotypes

    d) The Tories

(*The Face*, 53, September 1984)

The feature was called 'Role over – and enjoy it!' On one page was printed, manifesto-style, a series of pronouncements:

> The pop charts are full of boys dressed up as girls. The fashion magazines are full of girls looking like boys. The issue is not the bending of genders, it's the breaking down of sexual stereotypes. Women don't want to be seen in the stale, confining images. The new fetish, the new sex object, is men. (ibid.)

Laudable as this is in its claim that women don't want to be trapped in confining images, it is questionable whether the stratagem of simply replacing women by men in fashion spreads was much help to women. As it turned out the magazines' pictures of men marketed not a play on gender but an image of entrenched masculinity. *The Face* followed up this initiative with the Buffalo Boys (late 1984 into 1985), a series of photographs styled by Ray Petri which were sometimes fashion spreads and sometimes had a regular 'pin-up' spot. The look was very masculine, 'hard' and 'street'; the models were usually very beautiful men, often black or Hispanic; sometimes they were 'tough kids' like the child model Felix; always they wore 'street' clothes like Crombies, patent shoes, cycling gear and, nearly always, hats. Their captions added to the mythology:

> Portrait of a Buffalo Boy looking hard in the yard.

(*The Face*, 57, January 1985)

> Hard is the graft when money is scarce. Hard are the looks from every corner. Hard is what you will turn out to be. Look out, here comes a buffalo! 'The harder they come, the better' (Buffalo Bill).

(*The Face*, 59, March 1985)

Philippe un ami de Bruce, parlant buffalistiquement.

(*The Face*, 60, April 1985)

Float like a butterfly sting like a bee . . . Check out the beef!

(*The Face*, 62, June 1985)

Buffalo. A more serious pose.

(*The Face*, 77, September 1986)

Apart from being 'hard', Buffalo Boys were muscular and heavily built, a return to the masculine physique fashionable in the 1950s, before the skinny, pretty, hippy androgyne became fashionable in the 1960s. In the Buffalo photographs black men and, very occasionally, white women are represented as 'body', pure and simple, aestheticized but still an object rather than a subject. In effect masculinity replaced femininity as a commodity the fashion pages could work with. Where Boy George offered up femininity on the altar of fashion, and it was put to use by girls not boys, Buffalo Boys offered a representation of fetishized masculinity to both straight and gay men. These pictures are traps for the masculine gaze; a platonic aesthetic prevails which quite simply takes no account of women. A woman is free to look at them and enjoy them (as a man might enjoy looking at a fashion photograph of a woman) but they are not *addressed* to women. The type of photography exemplified by the Buffalo Boy simply puts men in the picture; it does not challenge the fundamental terms of traditional fashion photographs of women. Such pictures are iconic, devotional objects for private contemplation. The clothes are peripheral, the look is all: more than ever the fashion photograph sells 'dreams, not clothes' (Irving Penn, quoted Harrison, 1985, p. 13) but this time it sells the dream of perfect, seamless masculinity. The look was rapidly taken up by other fashion magazines and mainstream commercials. Bruce Weber photographed Olympic athletes like fashion models (*Interview* magazine, January–February 1983). The 'lost boys' of the fashionable world had come full circle, cast off their femininity, and recast their narcissism in a masculine mould.

In the early 1980s Blitz culture and the peacock male had put femininity on the map but kept it in their own hands. In the early to mid 1980s, a transitional stage, Boy George and 'safe' femininity competed with the street-credible and very

macho Bronx hip-hop culture. In the mid 1980s, the masculine won out over the feminine. Masculinity replaced femininity as a site of meaning in fashion and became incorporated into advertising, using a 1950s model of masculinity (for example the Brylcreem or Levis advertisements). This is, of course, over-schematic. Club culture continued, even more extravagantly, but was marginalized and lost its cutting edge. It moved from carnival to fancy dress, its emblems of misrule no longer potent.

In fashion imagery the juggling of gender manifested itself in an endless play on the idea of a viewer and an image that were sexually non-aligned – male/female/gay/straight. Such images replaced the more straightforward juggling of gender in the clubs by calling into question whom the image was *for*, to whose pleasure it was addressed. Robert Mapplethorpe produced a book of pictures of the woman body-builder Lisa Lyon (Mapplethorpe, 1983). Female body-building was seen to be fashionable rather than perverse. Body building gives definition to the body, it is a way of representing the body as an image of control; the ideal of muscular hardness connotes phallic definition. At the same time the cut of women's swimwear changed: the leg was cut very high, often above the hip bone (Plate 13). The high cut at the hips emphasizes the triangularity of the body, a classic masculine ideal silhouette, and the correspondingly longer, thinner section of the bathing costume covering the public region begins to resemble the shape of men's genitals. Thus the shoulders seem big (this corresponds to the fashion for big shoulder pads) and the hips are de-emphasized.

A British Gas shares advertisement in 1986 showed a black woman against a dark background in a white bikini, a body-builder with huge muscles. From a distance the figure read as a man but for the two white triangles covering her breasts, vestigial remnants of a femininity that the evolutionary process hasn't dealt with yet, like the little toe.

Plate 14 comes from a fashion spread in 1984 called 'Where the Buoys Are' in an issue of the *Tatler* devoted to gay culture. Here is the ultimate 'fashionalization' of transvestite dress, defused and deprived of its original meanings. It is far more convoluted than Annie Lennox or Boy George who made simple inversions which referred straightforwardly to the gender of the opposite sex. This image recalls Cocteau or Genet, a fantasy of Marseilles bars in the 1930s, an old-school male gay object of desire. Yet the model is a woman, the spread is 'for women' in that it shows women's fashions; the model is a woman trying to be a boy trying to be a woman. Dressed as a fantasy gay man, a trap for the homosexual gaze, she is a passive repository of desire. The picture, like Plate 13, follows Anthony Price's instructions

13. The triangular silhouette fetishized: black rubber swimsuit and gloves by Daniel James. Photograph by Herb Ritts from *Tatler*, April 1986. © The Condé Nast Publications Ltd

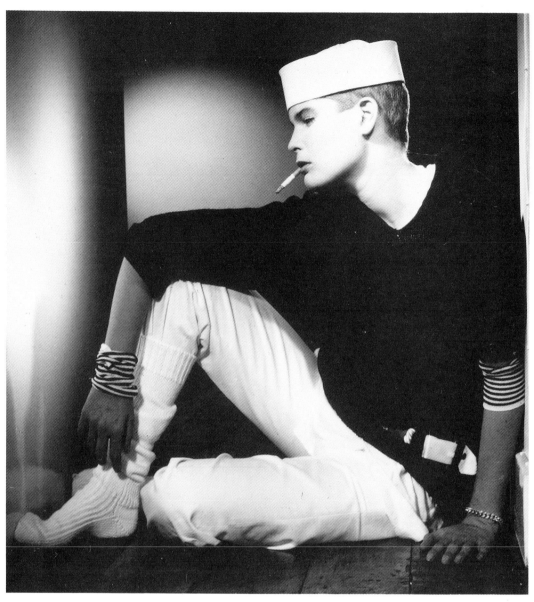

14. Confounding erotic categories: a woman model in a feature called 'Where the Buoys Are' from *Tatler*, February 1984. Clothes by Margaret Howell, hat by Caroline Charles. Photograph by Bruno Juminer © The Condé Nast Publications Ltd

(see above, pp. 44–6), a woman cast in the mould of a masculine fantasy. In the circus of gender juggling men win out over women and the phallus is reasserted as the gold standard that gives value to the currency of gender difference.

FOOTNOTES

1. Caroline Kellet documents this phenomenon in 'The Peacock Parade', *Vogue*, September 1983, p. 246. Good text and excellent pictures.

2. Flügel argues that men's bodily exhibitionism and narcissism is displaced on to women. In what he calls the Great Masculine Renunciation of the nineteenth century, men abandoned ornamental and luxurious clothing in favour of austere tailoring, which signified devotion to the principles of duty, renunciation and self-control. As a result the sole burden of being decorative was displaced, or projected, on to women (Flügel, 1930, pp. 110–13). In *The Theory of the Leisure Class*, first published in 1899, Veblen argues that the elaborateness of feminine apparel demonstrated women's exemption from labour and their obligation to consume, vicariously, for the head of the household (Veblen, 1953, Chapter 7).

3. This phrase inverts the terms of Flügel's Great Masculine Renunciation, ibid.

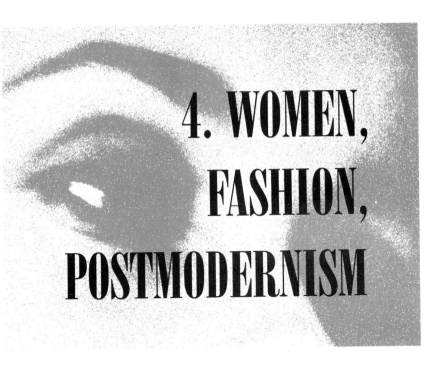

4. WOMEN, FASHION, POSTMODERNISM

BEDLAM

> . . . pure Fashion, logical Fashion . . . is never anything but an amnesiac substitution of the present for the past. We could speak of a fashion neurosis, but this neurosis is incorporated into a gradual passion, the fabrication of meaning: Fashion is unfaithful only in so far as it *acts out* meaning, *plays* meaning.

(Barthes, 1985, p. 289)

London fashion in the early to mid 1980s had a faster turnover of styles than ever before. Pirates, Buffalo Gals, New Romantics, rockabilly, new psychedelia, Hassidic ringlets, white dreadlocks, bobtails, Victorian fetish wear, zoot suits and Dickensian urchins erupted on to the streets. The 1930s, 1940s, 1950s and even the 1960s were cannibalized, recycled, refracted and sprinkled with Third World and ethnic references. The new design fever appeared to obliterate the cultural distinction between 'high' and 'low' which is exemplified in fashion by the distinction between 'designer' and 'street'. Since the decline in the 1960s of a seasonal 'look' of which women could be sure, mainstream fashion has deliberately constituted itself as a variety of 'looks'. But in the 1980s the turnover of looks speeded up hysterically. As a fashion caption in *The Face* put it in 1985: 'When the decadence of recent seasons crumbles in disorder (doesn't it always?) there will be no looks and no styles – only chaos. You might as well be in Bedlam . . .' (*The Face*,

65, September 1985). The picture (Plate 15), headed DESPAIR, *'acts out* meaning', *plays* despair, but it is ironic and self-parodying.

Avant-garde fashion became a field for parody, new looks which were also old in their reference to history, the cinema, traditional and folk culture, and to fashion itself. This development was paralleled in, and documented by, the newly recast fashion magazines in London, *i-D*, *The Face* and *Blitz*, 'where the life of the look is being lived'.[1] Barthes writes of 'the special temporality' of fashion, its 'vengeful present' which disavows the past and makes meaningless the signs of yesterday's fashion (Barthes, 1985, p. 289). Fashion, according to Barthes, abolishes long-term memory. In the early 1980s fashion's abolition of memory, and its 'infidelity' to the past, gave it a central place in the increasingly self-conscious emergence of postmodern culture.

Inside the back cover of the first issue of *i-D* magazine was an exhortation to readers:

OUT OF ORDER

Youth wore the hair of the Russian dissident, stance ska . . . Youth gleaned comfort from reference points in his past, used society's effluence creatively.

Youth searched through the tat stalls and Oxfam shops . . . Youth walked through the supermarket doors, humming the Pop Group's single: 'We are all Prostitutes'. One line stood out: 'Department stores are our new Cathedrals.' There he stood in his local church, asking himself – shall I 'pray' the supermarket game?

(*i-D*, 1, 1980)

At the heart of the new magazines was the idea that identity (*i-D*) is forged by appearance. At its inception in 1980 *i-D* was not a fashion magazine as such. Addressed to both sexes, its vox pop coverage of 'ordinary' people in their own clothes turned the street into a catwalk on which people 'modelled' their identities (Plate 16). Similarly the magazine *The Face*, also started in 1980, implies that people *are* their face, that this is their identity. It seemed as if the future predicted by Andy Warhol in which 'everyone will be famous for fifteen minutes' had come about, at least in spirit. New professions emerged: the stylists who forged these identities and the 'style editors' (a term invented by Peter York) who were arbiters of them. The fashion subcultures of the 1980s suggested that one's identity is a function of what

15. 'Despair': photograph by Martin Brading from *The Face*, 65, September 1985. Clothes by 3D and Richmond-Cornejo, tutu from Kensington Market

one consumes, and specifically of what one wears. It seemed to indicate that the individual has *only* her or his body to play with, produce, manufacture or customize.

Early issues of *i-D* indicate the terms of the new consumerism; they featured photographs of young Londoners accompanied by information about their names, the music and clubs they liked, and where their clothes came from (Plate 16). Tellingly, their occupations were in some issues given under the heading 'mode', such as 'MAL: Mode – Mal is a clothing designer and entrepreneur . . .' (*i-D*, 2, 1980), or 'GEORGE: Mode – I'm a budding celebrity, the immaculate conception' (*i-D*, 4, 1981), which accompanied an early picture of Boy George in a nun's habit. *i-D* went on to become a major commercial magazine. Its earliest issues heralded the peculiar centrality of fashion to postmodern culture in its representation of fashion as a field of both spectacle and surveillance.

Yet postmodern culture had changed the terms of that spectacle, that surveillance. Developments in information technology resulted in the free availability of a 'city' style, abolishing the idea of 'the provinces'. The nation, through video, television and magazines, became a vast metropolis as city style was disseminated through it. Microtechnology and computer-generated images, such as Max Headroom and some *i-D* fashion spreads and covers, were co-opted in fashion as a fantasy of the robot or automaton as 'personality', a fantasy which was underwritten by the idea of the body as a genetically coded machine. Such a body may be gendered but it is essentially manufactured rather than natural. The (essentialist) association between nature, identity and the body is disturbed when the idea of gender becomes coded rather than natural in fashion fantasy. The body can be made, through dress, to play any part it desires, as gender coding is displaced from the body on to dress.

In Blitz culture, boys moved in on 'femininity', not only on the territory of narcissism but also on female masquerade. In postmodern culture, gender was not so much manipulated for special effect as played with as just one term among many. In the new magazines, read by both sexes, sexual difference was used in fashion spreads as just another historic, folkloric, cinematic or fashion signifier. The consequences for women were varied: there might be a greater possibility for anonymity as a woman, since if gender is just one term among many the issue of difference recedes from the foreground. Alternatively, it might be possible to explore a more traditional 'womanliness' without being positioned as a 'traditional woman', again because the multiplicity of roles on offer make the role of 'femininity' less loaded, less immediate and less pressing. In a postmodern culture, where the categories of worth and worthlessness are easily inverted, fashion ceases to be marginalized as an

3

COLIN: Mode - Colin is wearing black pleated trousers which he made himself. The cardigan is from Marks and Spencers, £9.99 and the shoes from Axiom in the Kings Road, £5.99. Fave music - Siouxsie and the Banshees and David Bowie.

Wi-D!

STRAIGHT UP

Photographed by Steve Johnston

Anonymous girl with spiky hair-do.

16. The fashion magazine as identity parade: a page from the first issue of *i–D*, 1980. Photographs by Steve Johnston. Courtesy of *i–D* magazine

exclusively female preoccupation. Fashion, newly positioned in postmodern culture, itself positions women in new ways.

In Plate 17 three models pose in gawky, childlike attitudes wearing tutus and leather bomber jackets. It is not immediately clear what sex they are but the caption tells us they are women. The outfit consists of layers of masculine and feminine garments, down to the Doctor Martens customized with ribbons. Signifiers of sexual difference are superimposed on a body that is presented as androgynous and childlike. Much of the excitement of fashion imagery of this period, especially (as here) in those magazines aimed at both sexes, was achieved by the deployment of sexual difference as a pure signifier, detached from biological difference. In such images the play of clothing signifiers presented gender as just one term among many. However the *frisson* of excitement that accompanied these manipulations only existed because sexual difference waited in the wings, always ready to re-emerge as a 'naturalized' polarity – man or woman. Precisely because sexual difference was construed as old-fashioned, it could be recycled in postmodern fashion. The accumulation of such images worked to produce sexual difference as an anti-fashion symbol, part of an historic folk culture. As such it could be strategically ignored, or it could be 'fashionalized', brought back into fashion as yet another signifier of postmodernity.

THE DENIAL OF DIFFERENCE

Structurally, the junior is presented as the complex degree of the *feminine/mascu-line*: it tends towards androgyny; but what is more remarkable in this new term is that it effaces sex to the advantage of age; this is, it seems, a profound process of fashion: it is age which is important not sex.

(Barthes, 1985, p. 258)

In the early 1980s the currency of femininity was replaced by, or made interchangeable with, masculinity in the representations of subcultural style. But in a similar and parallel trend sexual difference was displaced altogether from the force field of fashion by the idea of the youthful consumer. Benetton produced a range of advertisements for children's wear under the slogan 'United Colours of Benetton'

17. Leather, studs and tulle. Photograph by Peter Moss from *Blitz* magazine, February 1986. Styling/concept by Iain R. Webb. Clothes from Johnsons, Lonsdale, Gamba and Classic Clothing

(styled by Caroline Baker, who had made her reputation as an innovative stylist in the new magazines) which juxtaposed 'kids' of all races bedecked with cultural or national emblems such as stars and stripes, hammers and sickles, and models of the world. While no doubt referring to the American Band-Aid single 'We Are the World', these advertisements created one big youthful happy family, a children-hold-hands-across-the-world ethic in which significant differences, of race, of class and of sex, were denied in a capitulation to 'Youth'. 'Youth' makes a perfect consumer group, a lesson learnt in the 1950s and increasingly capitalized on. Such images, with their glib and sentimental references to world peace and to children, deny the existence of conflict, be it of class, race or sex, in favour of an equalizing norm of consumerism of which the child becomes the very emblem.

i-D magazine also gave equal priority to men and women, it used black models, it showed people on the street and in clubs; but it was as if it used all this, like the Benetton advertisement, to distance itself from class conflict, racism or sexism. It adopted the format of the manifestos of the twentieth-century avant-garde to endorse the do-it-yourself ethic in fashion as an expression of individuality:

> We believe in the individual
> > in variety
> > individuals produce variety.

> (i-D, 2, 1980)

Individuality became another device to iron away significant difference. If we are all individuals and that fact is paramount then, in effect, we are all identical.

In the early 1980s the most important new designers made clothes for both sexes – Jean Paul Gaultier, Katherine Hamnett, Comme des Garçons, Vivienne Westwood, Yohji Yamamoto – marking a significant change. In London, as elsewhere, design teams of one man and one woman with more or less interchangeable roles were set up: Richmond/Cornejo, Crolla, Bernstock-Spiers, BodyMap. In their work the difference between designing for men or for women was no longer relevant. As a fashion issue it was relegated to the past: 'Men aren't any better than women or vice versa. We want to crash through the gender barrier. We make clothes that anyone can wear' (John Richmond of Richmond/Cornejo, quoted i-D, 39, August 1986).

18. Vestigial difference: an advertisement for Katherine Hamnett, 1984. Courtesy of *i–D* magazine and Katherine Hamnett

Similarly the marketing of fashion design proposed the male and female consumer as interchangeable. Plate 18 is an advertisement from 1984 for clothes by Katherine Hamnett. A black man and a white woman wear crumpled and baggy garments, vestigially differentiated. Masculine/feminine, black/white, become free-floating signifiers of fashionability, of up-to-date-ness, detached from any (possibly oppositional) political, cultural or sexual identity.

MAPPING THE BODY

If conventional ideas of sexual difference were out of fashion the body certainly was not. Indeed, it seems that the body itself has become the critical site of the struggle for (and against) meaning in contemporary culture. Again, fashion in the mid 1980s was ideally situated to play out this concern. The function of dress to define the body and to bring it into language is deliberately foregrounded in contemporary fashion. The male body too has been drawn into the fashion system and this changes the context in which women are represented in fashion.

In 1982 David Holah and Stevie Stewart set up BodyMap, a name which exemplified their approach. The name was taken from a piece by Italian artist Enrico Job who photographed sections of his own body and reassembled them in two dimensions, collaging the photographs together. 'it seemed to sum up our approach to pattern cutting' (David Holah, quoted in *The Face*, 61, May 1985). BodyMap clothes had holes in unexpected places which worked to shift the emphasis from one part of the body to another (mapping the body). Holah and Stewart were trying to explore new parts of the body and 'to amalgamate bits of flesh with bits of clothing and [to] try to make the two merge . . .' (David Holah, quoted in *i-D*, 21, December 1984–January 1985). BodyMap's clothes emphasized a phenomenological approach to the body. The traditional emphasis in fashion on both a standardized body and on sexual difference was obscured in favour of a less familiar enquiry into the body and its relation to clothes (Plate 19).

In contrast Georgina Godley in the mid 1980s turned her attention to the female form and the idea of womanliness. Her first solo collection was called 'Body and Soul' and featured a Body Dress, a Soul Dress and a Muscle Dress. The Muscle Dress had draped and pulled sections of jersey stitched on to the bodice to resemble sinews. (There are pictures of this collection in *The Face*, 71, March 1986, p. 36.)

19. The phenomenology of the body: a man and a woman model BodyMap clothes from a 1984 collection. Photograph by Chris Woode

Later collections included a hysterical pregnancy dress (padded to look as if the wearer was pregnant) and a wedding dress in which the panel over the breasts was cut out and replaced with a section of transparent gauze. In 1984, while still designing for Crolla, she used fruit-and-flower-patterned chintz. The work made conscious reference to symbols of female fertility within the context of a specifically English 'traditionalness'. Georgina Godley designed the clothes and herself styled Plate 20. Typically, it is a picture which one does not know whether to take seriously or not . . . a fashion image of a bride in boots glimpsed through a slit in a veil, staring reverentially at a phallus? The caption to a detail, reproduced on the opposite page, reads: 'the phallic dough cross and sceptre baked in the oven to be eaten at the nuptials'. The photograph scrambles the codes of 'bridal wear' yet it appears to insist on a feminine submission to the rituals of possession which is far more extreme than anything in *Brides* magazine. Sometimes it seems as if such representations are merely played off against the over-certainties of popular feminism. At other times they might propose a different reading of women's power and fashion as a place from which to confirm it.

The Georgina Godley bridal image presents a mixture of primitivism, traditionalism and sophisticated fashion. A feature of postmodernism is the way in which history is reduced to a series of evocative images, gestures and poses. In Frederic Jameson's formulation the past is evoked in a 'historicism' that effaces history, 'historicism' being 'the random cannibalization of all the styles of the past' (Jameson, 1984, p. 65). If history becomes a series of styles then fashion history may be seen as *the* historical model. Westwood and McLaren's Pirate collection of 1978 kicked off the practice of historical pastiche that became a feature of fashion in the 1980s, particularly in London. John Galliano's Fallen Angels collection of 1985–6 showed a meticulously researched variation of *Directoire* dress for women (Plate 21). Semi-transparent white muslin dresses were dampened with water as they had been in 1800 to cling to the body like the drapery of classical sculpture. The body was revealed again in the revival of a revival:

I didn't do the watersoaked muslin to shock anyone. It was just beautiful to see a woman walking down the catwalk and wearing this dress and to see the flesh move behind this film of gauze. It was never designed as a garment for someone to walk down the street in. We made silk slips to go under them and sold them as wedding dresses.

(John Galliano, quoted *City Limits*, 9–16 October 1986)

20. Fertility rites: bridal fashion designed and styled by Georgina Godley. Photograph by Marc Lebon from *i–D*, 22, February 1985

It is perhaps typical of contemporary fashion that clothes capable of making a connection between dress, the body and social change, between, as here, revelation and revolution, should confine their impact to the catwalk. The showcases of fashion – the catwalk and the fashion image – have an increasing autonomy. Outrageous fashion turns the street into a catwalk, the catwalk never turns into the street. Increasingly the catwalk is called the 'runway' – fashion launches itself into the international ether.

Both Godley and Galliano reacted against the youthful androgyny of early 1980s' fashion. Both made highly impractical clothing that, in a sense, defined itself as unfashionable, or against current trends. Their work did not parody or make jokes about the body but purported, against all the evidence, simply to show it. In the work of both there is an indication of a conscious resistance to the political implications of the work and a calculated insistence on the primacy of aesthetic considerations. Through the foregrounding of aesthetics their work finds a way to be serious in fashion, deliberately bracketing this seriousness in a discourse of folly.

In Paris the work of Jean Paul Gaultier exemplified the breakdown in contemporary fashion between high and street fashion. Dissociating himself from the high seriousness of a Galliano or a Godley, Gaultier referred to his love of kitsch, excess and waste:

I am not a genius, I am a *couturier*, I look around me all the time to see these B-movie things that happen, and I eat them all in. It just goes in and goes through the digestion, yes? Three years later it comes out of my bottom, and then I think 'Ah, yes, maybe this is good.'

(Gaultier, quoted *The Sunday Times*, 10 August 1986)

Gaultier used the semiotic playfulness and wit of subcultural fashion in a *couture* context. But if Gaultier is a postmodern couturier he is also a modern Schiaparelli, raiding the image bank and scavenging the world for imagery that can be subverted into surreal jokes. As in Schiaparelli's work, symbolic objects and clothing fetishes become toys. In a 1984 'Dervish bra', two tasselled fez hats form a strip-tease bra. His work made topical comments on the body in a culture of technological revolution. A jacket of 1979 was ornamented with *'broderie électronique'* and worn with tin-can bracelets. The electronic circuit became a decorative device on a bionic body. His Aran dresses of 1983 presented a more extended commentary on the

21. Revelation and revolution: dampened muslin dresses from John Galliano's Fallen Angels collection, autumn/winter 1986. Photograph by Chris Woode

female body. They were variations on tubes of creamy Aran Island knitting in which the traditional bobbles became nipples on knitted-in breasts – a piece of folksy genetic engineering. The Aran dresses made fun of one of the canonical distinctions of women's fashion, the distinction between country and town, chunky knits and sexual provocation. Gaultier used the tactics of subcultural fashion to make jokes at the expense of fashion orthodoxies, particularly those of Paris. Unlike many other contemporary designers, he dealt with the male body in the same terms as the female, designing a backless T-shirt for men and a backless leather biker's jacket, an acute conflation of narcissistic machismo (bikers) and feminine display (the backless dress).

Subculture infiltrated designer fashion in so far as the designing of clothes as statements became legitimate practice. In that move the illicit meanings of subcultural style as signifying practice changed. The dichotomy whereby fashion is identified with women and oppositional style with masculine subcultures was erased in postmodern fashion. Does this make a new space for resistance in women's fashion or does it undermine the oppositional possibilities of style?

THE BODY POLITIC

As a prominent discourse in postmodern culture dress may stand in as a billboard. Politics and fashion are no longer exclusive categories, the one serious and the other frivolous, as they had been seen for so long by both Left and Right. Indeed, as politics and fashion came closer together the old distinction between Left and Right itself seemed to shift. The cause of designer politics was made famous by Katherine Hamnett in London in 1983 when she produced a range of big silk T-shirts with messages in huge black letters such as CHOOSE LIFE, STOP ACID RAIN, EDUCATION NOT MISSILES and 58% DON'T WANT PERSHING. Hamnett herself wore the 58% DON'T WANT PERSHING slogan to Downing Street to be congratulated by Margaret Thatcher in 1984 when she won the British Fashion Industry Award for the Most Influential Designer of the Year.

Hamnett's T-shirts put fashion and politics together in a very uncompli-cated way. The straightforward alliance of fashionableness and social criticism seems, however, merely to counteract the subversive potential of both practices. Because such a move is straightforward, clear and direct both the politics and the fashion are constructed as inescapably liberal and bourgeois. The subversive potential of subcultural style lies in the indirectness of its utterances. The subcultural use of style as a system of signification is complex because it has to be: it is the mark of minorities that they establish their subcultural space by making their statements — verbal, sartorial and behavioural — opaque to the dominant culture: 'the challenge to hegemony which subcultures represent is not issued directly by them. Rather it is expressed obliquely, in style' (Hebdige, 1979, p. 17).

Within this scheme of things dress is significant precisely because it is a means of *indirect* communication and as such can hit, so to speak, below the belt. On the level of discourse, Westwood and McLaren's pornographic T-shirts of the 1970s, for which they were prosecuted, 'injured' their targets far more successfully than Hamnett's overtly political and ecological T-shirts. But on the other hand, on the level of economics, a proportion of the price of Katherine Hamnett's very expensive silk T-shirts was donated to organizations like Friends of the Earth and CND.

In a meticulously styled fashion spread in *The Face* (67, November 1985), models wear customized jewellery of anti-apartheid leaflets attached with paper clips and kilt pins (Plate 22). What sense can be made of such an image other than a purely aesthetic one? To whom is it addressed? Later *The Face* produced a 'Beirut Terrorists' spread that was more extreme but in many ways typical of current fashion's willingness to deploy any and all available material. Fashion has always peddled images to addicts. When history fails politics is plundered in the magazine's search both for meanings and for novelty.

In the early 1980s the relationship between high fashion and subcultural fashion shifted in an unprecedented way. Essentially the function of subcultural style as resistance to the dominant culture was obscured. Its function now appeared to be that of feeding high and mainstream fashion with a never-ending source of novelties. High fashion no longer despised subcultural style as both amateurish and tasteless but looked to it politely for inspiration. By the mid 1980s this symbiosis seemed complete; fashion was fashionable, and authentic gestures of resistance and refusal appeared to belong to the past.

In this development punk seems to have marked a turning point. Punk was a pivotal moment between modernist and postmodern sensibility. Punk was postmodern in its detachment of the signifier from the signified (for example in its use of the swastika), its insistence on the meaninglessness of its icons, and its use of pastiche and kitsch. But it was classically oppositional in that it evoked a political and social reality beyond itself. Punk's insistence on blankness, similar in some ways to a postmodern celebration of depthlessness, was nevertheless an oppositional

22. Meticulously styled politics. Clothes by Relief, styling by Caroline Baker. Photograph by Robert Erdman from *The Face*, 67, November 1985

stance. In postmodern culture, such oppositions multiply and dissolve: like a kaleidoscope, each shake produces another set of oppositions. Punk managed to be both blank *and* depthless, in a collision of authentic politics and postmodern sensibility. As such it was one of the most sophisticated and effective manifestations of subcultural power to 'resist through rituals'.[2]

In postmodern culture the relationship between ritual and 'reality' that post-war youth subcultures played on is disturbed, and with it the significance of the past. Frederic Jameson argues that the past, or history, has become, in the postmodern world, 'a vast collection of images, a multitudinous photographic simulacrum . . . the past as referent finds itself gradually bracketed, and then effaced altogether, leaving us with nothing but texts' (Jameson, 1984, p. 66).

This formulation of postmodern culture as being without a referent to a historical or contemporary reality is pertinent to an analysis of subculture. In Blitz culture the street and the catwalk were no longer distinguishable. *i-D* magazine photographed people on the street and reassembled them on the catwalk of the magazine. The traditional conflict between subcultural ritual and the referent of 'reality' was effaced. In terms of style there remained 'nothing but texts' (Jameson, ibid.), but some of these texts could be curiously resonant.

THE NOVEL OF FASHION

Sicilian sisters blown by the hot lusty winds of a corrupt Palermo, of murderous lemon groves. Like children who do not know the beauty they've grown into, they paint Sophia Loren eyes in axle grease. She wants to be as wild as her brothers and dance in the sulky nights with strange soldier boys like her sister. The seamed stockings, laddered from scrambling over walls in the dark, and the slip of a negligée are cast-offs from mothers who have retreated into the black of the church; the bandit jacket and mafioso's raincoat exchanged for a kiss as the bar closed. And in the tempestuous uncertain summer these freedom fighters hold on to themselves as if to control a speechless passion . . . baby!

(*i-D*, 33, February 1986)

This text introduces a fashion spread entitled 'Sicilian Freedom Fighters: Sophia

Loren slept in her make-up'. The text introduces the images in which two young women models wear clothes styled with string and rags against a faint grey background of enlarged layouts from the magazine. It accompanies the first image in the spread of a baby-faced model in close up, one eye closed, one ringed in black. She wears a black and white T-shirt into which is stuck a torn cardboard box. The layout credits models, stockists and photographer, but not the author of the text.

The postmodern characteristics of fragmentation, decentralization, inter-textuality and pastiche seem to find their apotheosis in that most exemplary text of marginality, the fashion caption. Mid-1980s fashion spreads were often accompanied by fragmented, allusive and cryptic quasi-literary texts. They resonated with meanings which they failed to utter. In Barthes' terminology, they do not denote, they connote.[3] They featured in sophisticated magazines yet they were frequently striking in the extent to which they designated teenage fantasy.

This elaboration was the latest historical development in this quintessentially marginal genre. It is to an analysis of the fashion caption, 'spoken Fashion', that Barthes devotes himself in *The Fashion System*. He discusses the ways in which the text communicates between the 'garment' and the 'world', for example in the phrase 'a sweater for chilly autumn evenings during a weekend in the country' (Barthes, 1985, p. 191). For Barthes, the rhetoric of the fashion caption creates a *tableau vivant*. He argues that the especial flexibility and ambiguity of the language of the fashion caption allows for a 'fashion novel' which is based on a collection of essential features comprising roles, models, situations and characters, and a loosely linked narrative. These roles are stereotypes of femininity: 'it is the stereotype which founds the equilibrium of Fashion's rhetoric' (ibid., p. 248). In his analysis fashion depends on stereotypes of women which it then seeks to reproduce. He talks of 'woman's identity . . . established in the service of man . . . of Art, of Thought' (ibid., p. 253).

But in the postmodern fashion text these stereotypes became scrambled, creating a fragmented, even schizoid, identity. In contrast, Barthes predicates a 'real' world of referents. In Barthes' analysis, 'Fashion communicates with reality, even if it stamps this reality with a constantly festive and euphoric mark' (ibid., p. 195). The magazines he analysed used a straightforward language: 'I am a secretary and I like to be impeccable' (ibid., p. 246). The fashion novel of the late 1950s and early 1960s, when Barthes wrote *The Fashion System*, was a kind of *roman à clef*: it referred to shopping, seaside holidays, country walks, sometimes to work. The novel of fashion in the 1980s had as its referent 'dressing up'. It was predicated not on the 'reality' which Barthes describes but on a fictional world of heterogeneity and the random play of signifiers. Jameson (1984) comments on the postmodern appetite for a world transformed into images of itself, for 'pseudo events' and spectacles. The caption to the fashion novel of the 1980s created not a *roman à clef* but an anti-realist novel, a fantastical one. It might be historical romance, detective story, science fiction or even a horror story. A make-up feature in *i-D* (33, February 1986) showed gory wounds on the faces of two models, drawn from the special effects department rather than the cosmetics counter.

There was a connection here between the effacement of the referent in contemporary culture and the way in which the marginal discourse of the fashion caption constructed a world. In the 1980s the referent of avant-garde fashion was a fictionalized 'elsewhere' rather than the traditionally social world of fashion, complete with familiar stereotypes of femininity, although these still existed in more conventional magazines such as *Vogue*. The privileging of fashion in contemporary culture may be a function of the way in which the 'fictionalized' world of fashion exemplifies a postmodern hyperreality.[4]

Returning to the text from *i-D*, the fictional world that it sets up and into which we are to insert both models and garments pictured is also in some sense a feminized one. Within its terms, the feminine and the infantile are conflated. In Barthes' analysis the fashion text cannot 'achieve' literature because literature is what it signifies. Here the scattered text refers to cinematic narratives and to the literature of, simultaneously, the modernist novel, the trashy paperback, the pornographic narrative and women's romantic fiction. Ultimately we are in the world of fantasy, here of infantile fantasy ('. . . baby!')

Commenting on the especial tone of the fashion caption Barthes writes:

> It is possible that the juxtaposition of the excessively serious and the excessively frivolous, which is the basis for the rhetoric of fashion, merely reproduces, on the level of clothing, the mythic situation of women in Western civilization, at once sublime and childlike.
>
> (Barthes, 1985, p. 242)

In the text from *i-D* passion and freedom come together with eye make-up and raincoats in an elliptical narrative. Religion, sibling rivalry and jackets are all juxtaposed in the name of the infantilized and fragmented 'feminine'. The text demonstrates the continuum in the representations of postmodern culture between fashion, infantilism, passivity and femininity. The *i-D* spread manipulates these connections with an ambiguous knowingness. In postmodern fashion we are again and again confronted by the interaction of the sophisticated and the infantile, by a 'feminized' conjunction of the sublime and the childlike. As the critical and creative practices of postmodern culture are marked by the deliberate negotiation of depthlessness and superficiality, in fashion 'the feminine', as a text, a code, divorced from nature and history, becomes the site for postmodern fashion's 'acting out' of meaning.

FOOTNOTES

1. This phrase was used to describe the new magazines by Dick Hebdige in a lecture on postmodernism in 1986 at the Central School for Art and Design in London.
2. For the seminal account of resistance through ritual see Hall, Clarke, Jefferson and Roberts (eds), 1976.
3. The distinction is made in *Camera Lucida* (Barthes, 1984).
4. Baudrillard describes the concept of simulation as 'the generation by models of a real without origin or reality: a hyperreal' (Baudrillard, 1983, pp. 1–2).

5. WOMEN SURVEYING WOMEN: DEVIANT CONSUMERS

I have here in front of me a series of fashion plates . . . These costumes, which many thoughtless people, the sort of people who are grave without true gravity, find highly amusing, have a double kind of charm, artistic and historical.

(Baudelaire, 1981, p. 391)

We have here a series of fashion plates, not a history of fashion photography but a personal selection of six photographs, each accompanied by an essay, a series of meditations on a hobby horse. These hobby horses range from a consideration of fantasy and the subjective pleasures for women of looking at fashion photographs, to how women picture themselves, position themselves, and are themselves positioned by fashion imagery.

The fashion image as a genre is under-theorized, possibly because it is difficult to discuss a system of representations whose essence lies in transitoriness. Baudelaire defends the fashion image *as* image in his essay *The Painter of Modern Life* but in general those writers who have analysed fashion have not specifically addressed the fashion image.[1] More recently however, and particularly since the 1970s when fashion photography became more highly imbued with narrative and sexual content, there have been some important analyses, particularly by women.[2] This writing has informed the inclusion of the photographs by Helmut Newton (Plate 23) and

Deborah Turbeville (Plate 24) whose work formed part of a shift in the content of the fashion image, a shift which attracted the scrutiny of a feminist enquiry into representations of women.

Fashion imagery like fashion in general, tends to be trivialized. This trivialization works to further the transitoriness of the fashion image. It becomes doublecoded, simultaneously trivial and transgressive, and the slippage between the two is capable of calling both categories into question.[3] Fashion takes its revenge against its trivialization: it gets away with murder. Extraordinary liberties are taken precisely because it is 'only' fashion. The 'evidence' lies in the photographs themselves which are, like all good mystery stories, the stuff of high drama, tragicomedy, melodrama, satire or, even, burlesque. Violence may be a theme, but so are pleasure, desire, comedy, even depression. Here the outrageous, or the transgressive, particularly in relation to female sexuality, find covert expression. The cover provided by fashion's trivialization marks it out as a cultural space in which 'femininity' is both made and unmade.

It is generally assumed that women look at or read fashion magazines to find out what is currently in fashion and how they can get hold of the relevant clothes or otherwise simulate the look in question. But the fashion image, particularly in the high fashion magazine, is also an object of consumption in its own right. Women read fashion magazines in a number of different ways – either for the clothes, the 'look', or for the image. The image may be perused as icon, or as a vehicle for fantasy, as well as for visual information about the clothes themselves. The high fashion or avant-garde fashion magazine, from which the following images are taken, is a magazine in which fashion is foregrounded as an autonomous discourse. The high or avant-garde fashion magazine does not seek to justify fashion or fashion's arbitrariness, its 'uselessness'. It might therefore be thought to present 'pure' fashion if such a thing is possible.

Fashion's representations are marginalized, fragmented, semantically elusive. To some extent these qualities are lost when the pictures are anthologized, or reproduced in a book like this, without captions, details about the clothes, a setting of the glossy magazine, with its own protocols and hierarchies. Here the pictures, separated from caption, text, the paraphernalia of the magazine, are cut off from their only anchor, isolated from their context.

Magazines do not explicitly advertise or sell the clothes they feature in their fashion pages. The fashion magazine purports to represent a commodity – fashion – but in fact seeks to sell only itself – a look, an image, a world. This slippage is paralleled by a deviant, or perverse, consumption of the fashion image on the part of the reader. The women who cut their desire to the measure of the magazine image, practise a form of consumption that is both compliant and deviant. Women appear to be doing something with the images that they were not intended for, or not wholly intended for. Women do with these images both less and more than was intended. They may not (be able to) buy the clothes but they nevertheless consume the images. The question is *how*?

What do women want from images of women? What pleasure is at stake? Perhaps desire is determined by custom, by usage. The customs implicit in fashion photographs may at the same time prescribe women's fantasies or desires *and* permit a free space in which women map them for themselves. The following pieces were constructed to identify, or designate, some of the practices involved in this 'deviant' consumption.

'WORLD WITHOUT MEN'
(Helmut Newton, Plate 23)

World without Men is the title of an anthology of Helmut Newton's fashion photographs from the 1970s. Newton's work aggressively sexualizes the fashion image, seizing on its sensational possibilities; it is always informed by the theme of sexual power. Most typically the women in his photographs, encased in the hard gloss that seals the whole image, are tall, imperturbable, dominating. The pictures have their own logic, and it is a masculine logic deliberately imposed on the 'feminine' genre of the fashion photograph. The highly 'set up' quality of Newton's photographs speaks the photographer's dominance over the models for all their phallic pretentions. Newton highlights his own manipulative intervention into the supposedly feminine world of fashion by making the sexual content of that intervention explicit.

Plate 23 poses two women models in a crowded beach scene, Cannes possibly. In the foreground one model, in a semi-transparent black swimsuit and wrap flashes at another seated model who wears a cocked hat with a veil. This gesture is watched by two men, sitting among the oblivious crowds on the beach. The image centres around the flashing model's gesture and, in particular, on her *lack*; the action becomes doubly outrageous and shocking both for her phallic aggression and for her castration.

23. Overleaf. 'World without men'. Photograph by Helmut Newton from French *Vogue*, 1981. Clothes by Jean Barthet, Revillon and Yvan & Harzion

The act of flashing, a form of sexual exhibitionism, is associated with men. Exhibitionism, however, is not absent from the fashion image itself, or from the actual wearing of fashionable clothes. Newton's image, typically, seizes on the perverse implications of the routine exhibitionism of fashion modelling. Transposing the act of flashing from man to woman throws up an array of new meanings that centres around the absence of the penis which would validate the gesture. Rather than emptying the gesture of meaning altogether the transposition splinters and deflects its meanings. Her legs are open and bent, her hips thrust forward. The pose is both vulnerable and aggressive. In masculine fantasy, the sexually aggressive lesbian figure makes the same gesture as the sexually aggressive man, confirming his power in her pretensions to it. All of this is simultaneously subsumed in the image under the heading of a (bad!) practical joke, loony models on the job.

Fashion details keep pace with the outrageous content of the image. The transparency of the model's swimsuit reveals her breasts, a detail which confirms both her exhibitionism and her femininity. The theme of castration gives added piquancy to the diamanté flowers appliquéd on to the swimsuit: the eye moves from the dark gap between her legs to this curious decoration. It is the task of the fashion photographer to highlight the details of the garment in question (swimsuit by Yvan and Harzion). This function of the fashion image makes Newton's loaded themes gratuitous in a way that he exploits to the full.

The flasher's victim is marked by her severe detachment, her aloof control. She is at once victim of the situation and vying with the other for control of it. She is the intellectual to her madwoman (the copy of *Le Film Français*), the 'lady' to her 'whore', the man to her woman (the buccaneer hat). Sexual confrontation resolves itself into a struggle for power, in which each woman juggles with dominance and submission.

Two men look on. The image constructs the fashion model as a kind of hysteric and fashion as a hysterical discourse. The heightened appearance and gestures of the models make them surreal figures in the casual setting. They are screened off by 'fashion', locked in a dubious narrative that bears little relation to reality. To the right of the image a couple are caught in shot, an Adam and Eve to set against the conflicted sexual identity of the two fashion models. The make-believe of fashion here constructs itself around the make-believe of the flashing model, the multiple phallic pretensions played out in this little psychodrama.

The two closest male onlookers mirror our own gaze as observers. The questioning voyeurism of their gaze corresponds obliquely to our own problems in reading the image and confirms our own voyeurism. The presence of 'real' men adds another dimension to the phallic drama enacted by the female protagonists, emphasizing in particular the flashing model's make-believe.

Generally in Newton's work the conventional categories – fashion, pornography – are disturbed. The pornographic themes continually call into question whether the image is assembled for a male or a female viewer. Fashion photography, as in this image from French *Vogue*, usually addresses women – they are the supposed consumers of the clothes and the image. For all its bewildering gratuitousness there is a narrative logic to this image, a point of view expressed. The logic of the picture is the logic of a male fantasy of lesbianism enacted for male pleasure. This phenomenon is more readily associated with pornography than with fashion pictures. How then is the woman viewer positioned here?

Newton's fashion photographs appear to address a female viewer who enjoys both the phallic pretence of the female models and also the suggestion of a male intervention on the part of the photographer which requires the 'models' to enact gestures of dominance. Perhaps, too, such images rely on the female viewer's vulnerability as one who looks defensively, in the sense that she does not wish to recognize herself as prudish or easily shocked. Here again is evidence of the fashion image's power to get away with murder.

Newton, by pushing against the barriers of what was acceptable in the fashion image revealed something of the workings of the genre. The aggressive sensationalism of his work and that of fellow photographer Guy Bourdin in the early 1970s countermanded the idea of fashion photographs as harmless images for women and brought a new and often disturbing edge to fashion photography.

Many women have found his work deeply offensive for its manipulative portrayal of women. As a fashion photographer Newton came to prominence at a time when the femininist critique of the representation of women in pornography and advertising was being elaborated. Newton's work was singled out from that of other photographers for its sadistic themes. Its affiliations with pornography were stressed to counteract the protected 'art' status of the high fashion image. Clearly Newton always seeks to be outrageous. It is the fashion photograph, supposedly a relatively innocent genre, that repeatedly furnishes the context for this outrageous-ness. The more outrageous sexual themes of Newton's work are played out in a sexualized portrayal of women's relationship to each other. Photographing women for fashion plates he is always able to touch a nerve of taboo that is, perhaps, inherent in the genre of fashion photography as a highly circumscribed 'world without men'.

'NARRATIVE PURGATORY'
(Deborah Turbeville, Plate 24)

The exact circumstances are, to us the viewer, unknowable . . . we know the ambience of the situation but never its pertinent facts. We sense the luxury, the sensuality, but the plot is rarely spelt out to us. The pose remains frozen in a narrative purgatory. Free of confining specifics, it is lost in that dream world where reality is negotiable. The fashion photograph becomes the image of promises. Through contextual ambiguity, the viewer (consumer) is seduced.

(Shottenkirk, writing about Robert Mapplethorpe, *ZG*, 9, 1983)

Like Newton, Deborah Turbeville worked largely for American *Vogue* in the 1970s, although her work also appeared in English *Vogue*. Her famous Bath-house series was paired in the same issue of US *Vogue* with Newton's photographs for *The Story of O-h-h* . . . Both photographers use narrative tableaux to create a sense of drama, an event, or a relationship between two models. Neither Newton's nor Turbeville's work would have been possible without the changes introduced in the 1960s by Guy Bourdin, who used mystery and suggestion to shift the fashion photograph from a static image towards a more dynamic, narrative one.

Yet Turbeville never achieved the same degree of notoriety as Newton; where his work is noisy, hers is quiet. His images are taut, hers are fluid. In the work of both, the fashion image is overloaded with narrative meanings which seem disproportionate to its significance as a fashion photograph. They differ drastically however in their representation of women, specifically in the way women are constructed in and by the narrative. Newton's pictures are overdetermined, layered densely with meanings about power; Turbeville's pictures are ambiguous, apparently loosely knit together, often refusing to make meanings at all.

By subordinating the fashion itself and venturing into a vague borderline area between clarity and confusion, Turbeville questions the very basis of fashion photography and subverts the traditional idea that fashion should be shown clearly.

(Hall-Duncan, 1979, p. 217)

Most of her photographs are of women, in pairs or groups, in interiors. In all her

24. 'Narrative purgatory'. Photograph by Deborah Turbeville, 1980, for the Thierry Mugler collection. This photograph appears in *A Strange Tale of Ivan P*, a 1988 photonovella by Deborah Turbeville

work she fetishizes a certain type of interior: the distressed wall, the unidentifiable space full of urban detritus, the wash-house, the studio, the grand empty house, the derelict workspace. She has colonized such spaces to produce a sense of poetic loss, a no-man's-land inhabited by women alone (Plate 24). Within this interior, women enact inactivity. They are sad, beautiful, self-regarding, hermetically enclosed. Their eyes are downcast, or they stare distractedly into space. They slouch, to the point where the slouching posture became one of the hallmarks of Turbeville's style (Hall-Duncan, 1979, p. 216). They rarely look at each other and never at the spectator. Turbeville writes:

> The photographs are like the women you see in them. A little out of balance with their surroundings, waiting anxiously for the right person to find them, and thinking that perhaps they are out of their time. They move forward clutching their past about them, as if the ground of the present may fall away. Their exteriors seem walled up and introverted; the interiors endless . . . airless. The very print quality reflects something in the women that is hesitant, a little faded and scratched; or that, having emerged into a light too harsh, stand frozen in space, over-exposed.

> (Turbeville, 1978, p. 1)

Their ambience is one of existential *weltschmerz*, of despair and alienation. Yet it is fashion which galvanizes them, which is their *raison d'être*. These pictures, with their apathetic, even depressive, figures, attack or block the bright breeziness and spurious dynamism of much fashion imagery. Again, the trivial is invested with significance, so that these figures are both fashion models and models of passive resistance. If, rarely, they look at another person, it is blindly, unseeingly. They refuse to engage. In a fashion narrative the gaze of the model makes sense within the logic of the picture; but these models refuse to endorse the logical fiction. They do nothing but be: be beautiful, be decorative, be alienated, be in a photograph they cannot escape from, be there to be looked at. They are models of intransitivity and they seem not to care, they disdain to put on a show of model-world 'real life'.

In Plate 24 two women inhabit the space to the side of a grand Parisian staircase, a transitional space in which they have come to a halt. The figure on the left is draped, hyperbolically, over the ironwork of the stair rail. Her pose is one of extreme despair or exhaustion. To her right stands a second, ambiguous figure who clutches the stair rail, her eyes downcast, most of the dress she models concealed by the staircase. They slouch. They do not look at each other. Their relationship, their presence in the house, are unexplained, mysterious. They are inert, mute. The poetics of the image lie in a refusal to use language to name or explain. If the symbolic is the realm of language these women insistently inhabit the imaginary, a world outside discourse, and in so doing put their 'reality' into question. There is a weird slippage in the narrative: things have gone wrong, or not right, but not explicably so. The image reads like a fantasy in which the vestigial thread of narrative has been lost. It has yet to achieve even the coherence, or the organization of fantasy. If the suggestion of a forceful narrative galvanizes Newton's images, in Turbeville's work the models pose like the shipwrecked survivors of a lost narrative.

In Turbeville's work this sense of slippage, this poetic rupture with both time and place suffuses the image. Again, the question comes to mind, where does such an image, lyrical and despairing, stand in relation to fashion? The picture, so divorced from a past or a future, is ultimately withholding, teasing. The spectator is invited to infer a meaning which cannot be grasped, to be the subject of a desire which cannot be gratified.

Refusing definition, Turbeville's women resist the phallicism which characterizes Newton's work. Her images are evocative, elusive. They are rarely clear. Without ever becoming wispy they avoid the hard edge of so much fashion photography. In a series of photographs from Turbeville's book *Wallflower* (1978) the women are crumbly, flakey, wrapped in plaster of Paris or bandages. She fakes old age by scratching the print. The image thereby becomes lost, irrecoverable via a reference to a spurious past that never was, as if the negative no longer existed and all that remained was a damaged print.

In Plate 24 the picture is soft, grainy, the tonal range narrow. The soft weight of the model draped on the bannister is counterpointed by the curtain that blows gently behind her. The photographer's presence is perhaps most evident in the disposition of the bodies; their organization within the frame is calculated, highly stylized. Helmut Newton in the 1970s habitually photographed shop-window mannequins to resemble women; Turbeville photographed women as wound-down dolls, broken marionettes.

In Turbeville's work the female body is passive, her women are hesitant, even depressive. But they embody a willed resistance: a resistance to fashion, to the gaze, to representation itself. In this way she subverts the genre of fashion photography: hiding the face, blurring the clothes, suggesting nothing better than a non-space in which to wear them. Her work suggests the fashion image as a space for a fantasy of tenuous sensuality, non-dress and passive drama that nevertheless refuses to form itself. It suggests the possibility of a fantasy without disclosing what it might be.

THE PHALLIC MOTHER
(Peter Lindbergh, Plate 25)

Plate 25 shows a fashion image from French *Vogue* in which a strikingly tall model in a suit by Jean Paul Gaultier walks towards the viewer; holding a cigarette in one hand, she elegantly pushes a pram with the other. The photograph gives her a hard, lean edge. In emphasizing her height and her silhouette, the image constructs her as a phallic presence. Yet the picture does not reproduce the stale terms of hackneyed male fantasy; rather, it generates a whole new scenario in which the woman is an active subject. In this highly stylized and witty presentation, the figure combines the entirely contradictory attributes of the dandy and the mother.

The picture is a neat contradiction built on a very rich one. Her phallicism is counterposed by the pram, a symbol of maternity which is otherwise denied. The garment she wears is tailored, with big shoulders and narrow hips, stressing the triangularity of the ideal masculine silhouette. Flügel talks of tailoring as phallic: 'both stiffness and tightness are, however, liable to be over determined by phallic symbolism . . . in general those male garments which are most associated with seriousness and correctness are also the most saturated with a subtle phallicism' (Flügel, 1930, pp. 76–7).

Like the nineteenth-century men's clothing which Flügel described, her suit is tailored, austere and lacking in extraneous detail, its only ornament a chain from nipple to nipple. The watch chain, that most masculine of ornaments, is wittily displaced here to connote toughness, nipple piercing, and tribalism; it pin-points the breasts themselves, otherwise barely noticeable, written out of this scenario.

The pram, with its contents which we cannot see, is both the code and the key to the picture. It constructs her simultaneously as mother and model, a representation of contradiction. In one possible scenario – the fashion shoot – the pram is clearly empty, co-opted as a fashion accessory for the woman who is clearly a

25. The phallic mother. Photograph by Peter Lindbergh, courtesy of French *Vogue*, August 1985. © The Condé Nast Publications Ltd. Clothes by Jean Paul Gaultier

model not a mother. In an alternative scenario, the logic of the picture, she is a mother pushing a baby down the street. In psychoanalytic theory, motherhood, far from being the graceful resignation to femininity of popular mythology, involves the mother's unconscious substitution of the baby for the phallus she lacks. At some level this image evokes such a proposal as both self-evident and amusing. She is a 'bad' mother.

She walks not on the pavement but in the road, putting her baby's life at risk by walking the wrong way up a one-way street. Smoking carelessly, she holds her cigarette above the pram which she seems to be using as an ashtray. She evokes the wicked nanny of films, a macabre and glamorous figure. Returning to the first scenario, in which the pram is empty, simply reinforces her 'badness'. There is something shocking in using a baby carriage as an accessory: it bears witness to the wicked frivolity of the woman of fashion who will exploit even the sacred rites of motherhood for the sake of novelty.

The pram, empty and sinister, recalls those narratives in which prams are used to transport dangerous items, bombs, secretly across enemy lines, all of which seems quite possible in view of her consummate failure to display any of the stereotyped characteristics of the mother. Symbolically, the baby is denied in every respect by the mother and her accoutrements. The pram becomes a surrealist object, an empty vessel, both literally and metaphorically. It may be a coffin, an ashtray, a pram or a fetish as it substitutes for a baby which substitutes for her lack. The hard-edged quality of the picture seems to spring from a kind of (masculine) overcompensation: garment and pram, tailoring and engineering, are all hysterical symptoms of a lack, empty shells.

Her clothes suggest the anonymity of uniform but the combination of austerity with elegance indicates the dandy. The style conveys an aloof autonomy which is not a quality associated with mothers pushing prams. The image plays on the distinction between the strategic anonymity of the dandy and the everyday high-street anonymity of the women who push prams. The iconic impossibility of a dandified mother is here made possible in the elaborate artifice of the fashion image. Baudelaire calls the dandy 'the man, finally, who has no profession other than elegance' (Baudelaire, 1981, p. 419). Here, is a mother, without a profession but with – the critical difference – elegance. Herein lies her transgression.

Ironically, the fashion photograph is a particularly suitable vehicle for this depiction of the transgressional woman. This picture of a quirky, dandified mother, unwittingly points to an unexplored area, the relation of fashion to maternity. High fashion tends to define itself against the maternal. In modern myth and stereotype the maternal body is dissociated from the qualities of glamour and sexiness which fashion endorses. This dissociation goes deeper than fashion's emphasis on youth or the supposition that fashion signals a female availability which is abandoned with maternity. In cultural stereotypes maternity and glamour, or the feminine will to power, are incompatible. In so far as fashion does sanction a feminine will to power it excludes the maternal.

Psychoanalytic theory uses the concept of the phallic mother to describe the child's pre-oedipal fantasy of a mother with a penis, an autonomous and all-powerful being. Just as the child is later forced to abandon this fantasy, so in adult culture the figure of the powerful and sexual mother is repressed. To posit the sexual mother is to posit her as both desiring subject and desired object; it is to recognize her independence, as well as the fact of her maternity, a dual contradiction which escapes the monolithic structures of stereotyping. The concept of the phallic mother works against the sentimentalization of motherhood. It counteracts a given misrepresentation and suggests a greater complexity in the relationship of mother to child.

But when fashion defines itself in opposition to the maternal perhaps it protests too much. Flügel discussed the unconscious association of clothes and dressing with the mother's love, and with its threatened loss. Attitudes to clothes are an unconscious reflection of feelings towards the maternal figure who dresses the child and to her protective function. Not surprisingly, these attitudes may also express conflict or contradiction.

For women, might fashion's most potent lure be an invitation to act out at the level of fantasy the relation of mother to daughter, a reflexive, mirroring relation in which the body is the central term? Perhaps the contemplation of the fashion image replicates or echoes this relationship. If so, how does fashion position women? Is it always as the daughter?

THE NEUROTIC IMAGE
(Sheila Metzner, Plate 26)

At the awkward age the girl is torn between the wish and the refusal to display herself.

(de Beauvoir, 1972, p. 543)

The space of this photograph (Plate 26) is curiously shallow, in strong contrast to the deep focus of Plate 25. It is the space of a showcase, in which the model becomes an exhibit, a collector's item. She is transfixed against the wall like a butterfly on a pin, her skirt held out in a gesture that is at once calculating and compulsive, part toreador, part victim. But for the fashion model, a workmanlike narcissism is part of the job – workwomanlike. If the model in this picture is an exhibit she also exhibits herself.

Beneath the straightforwardness of the shot and the familiar provocative, blank gaze of the model, there lurks a quality of uncertainty. In appearance half woman and half child, she wears the golden clothes which represent both the feminine body as finished object and the theatrical glitter which draws small children. The image captures a disjunction between the construction of the model as subject – self-exhibiting – and as object – exhibited. This disjunction generates the neurotic quality of the image.

Flügel argues that our attitude to clothes is essentially ambivalent:

. . . we are trying to satisfy two contradictory tendencies by means of our clothes, and we therefore tend to regard clothes from two incompatible points of view – on the one hand, as a means of displaying our attractions, on the other hand, as a means of hiding our shame. Clothes, in fact, as articles devised for the satisfaction of human needs, are essentially in the nature of a compromise; they are an ingenious device for the establishment of some degree of harmony between conflicting interests. In this respect the discovery, or at any rate the use, of clothes, seems, in its psychological aspects, to resemble the process whereby a neurotic symptom is developed. Neurotic symptoms, as it is the great merit of psychoanalysis to have shown, are also something of a compromise, due to the interplay of conflicting and largely unconscious impulses.

(Flügel, 1930, pp 20–21)

26. The neurotic image. Photograph by Sheila Metzner from British *Vogue*, December 1985. © The Condé Nast Publications Ltd. Clothes by Giorgio Armani

Plate 26, in its uncertainties, even its lack of conviction, evokes that ambivalence, the precariousness of that 'compromise'. Flügel suggests that the child's impulse towards self-display, its bodily narcissism and exhibitionism, are 'lured' from the naked to the clothed body where they can gratify themselves with less opposition. Plate 26 seems to have interrupted the girl/child in this process. Part of the infantilism of the model's pose lies in the sense that the displacement is incomplete, or blocked, an instance of childish resistance. Her almost exposed breast and tousled hair are at odds with the tractable way she holds out her skirt.

Despite its references to the young girl's passage from childhood to maturity – a coming-out ball? a present in gold wrapping paper? – the photograph is not sentimental nor is it a sympathetic image. In this picture of a somewhat troubled spoilt brat there is no moral at all. A conscious amorality is often a characteristic of the fashion photograph. The rhetoric of its supposed frivolity frees it from moral constraints, even from having to mean anything at all. Regarding this picture's lack of sentimentality it is perhaps significant that the photographer is a woman. The conflicts involved in the business of becoming a woman are often such as to preclude sentimentality from a woman's account of them. The image evokes the difficulty of feminine self-determination and the possibility, for women, of control over the representation of their own bodies. It goes further, and makes a spectacle of this impasse.

References to childhood are provoked by the apparent youth of the model. In both the 1960s and the 1980s fashion models have often been very young. This is, in part, an instance of fashion's rejection of the mature female body which reflects the fear and repugnance it evokes in contemporary Western culture. The use of very young models, however, also evidences the infantilized and infantalizing nature of fashion. Seen in this light fashion is playful, indulgent, amoral and unable to transcend its somatic preoccupations; all this is coextensive with its particular brand of sophistication and worldliness. However, within the crass infantilism of fashion there are discernable echoes of the forgotten psychic world of childhood. Fashion's unconscious infantilism, combined with its preoccupation with clothes and the body, point to it as a discourse in which the primary but elusive experience of the body in infancy may be rearticulated.

If dress is implicated in social codes and language it is also bound up with the body, with a pre-verbal consciousness and with a certain resistance to language. This double articulation gives clothing a place in both the symbolic and the imaginary, a privileged position which makes dress and clothing a rich area of investigation. Perhaps it is particularly so for women, for whom the experience of their own bodies has been so hard to articulate. What of the role of clothes in the little girl's experience of her body? And what of their role in the precarious development of a feminine identity? Such considerations refer back to the image in hand.

Despite the grand setting, the Armani skirt and scarf-wrap in gold silk organza do not connote sophisticated fashion so much as childish 'dressing up', a glitzy princess costume for masquerading. This 'princessiness' secures for the image its association with fairytales, narratives in which the girl makes her transition to grown-up femininity and finds her prince (*Cinderella*, *The Sleeping Beauty*). But here the narrative is fissured, its sequence collapsed in a single neurotic image. She holds out her skirt like a good girl but her messed up hair and over-made-up lips connote the excessive sexuality of the bad girl. The controlled representation of femininity is threatened. The neurosis of the image suggests a body which cannot be represented coherently, a body that is in conflict with representation, with dress, with *the* dress.

Gesture, costume and gaze can evoke different moments of feminine sexual awareness that form an elliptical narrative of the daughter's transition to womanhood: the identification with her mother and her rivalry with her, the wished-for seduction of the father, waiting for the prince. She, the feminine model, is a blank on which to inscribe the confused autobiography of one's own femininity, with its sub-plot of resistance and refusal. It is a story with no moral (and very little justice), that involves a body, a dress and a mirror. Such a reading constructs the fashion photograph as an illustration to a deviant or neurotic narrative of femininity, a reading which is at odds with the conventional idea of fashion imagery as an exhortation to feminine conformity.

Returning to the shallowness of the image, its compressed and confined space is an intrinsic part of its representation of feminine self-display. Perhaps the unsettling quality of the image lies in its own lack of conviction, and in its unconvincingness as a vehicle of any depth. Contradictory signs are accumulated to suggest conflict in a form, the fashion photograph, which cannot accommodate it, which has no depth. Within this reading the photograph, as an enactment of feminine self-display, may be understood as symptomatic: femininity is a masquerade, a matter of dressing up, but it is also a costume that must be worn with conviction – for real. Femininity is constructed as both surface and depth.

The fashion image is at once empty and overdetermined. To read it as a woman is to supply meaning through recognition. Judith Williamson discusses the kaleidoscopic version of femininity in Cindy Sherman's work, describing the cultural construction of femininity as 'multiple, fractured . . . yet each of its infinite surfaces gives the illusion of depth and wholeness' (Williamson, 1983, p. 106). In Plate 26, with its flattened quality and its attention to surface, that illusion is subtly undermined. Williamson suggests that the viewer is 'forced into complicity with the way these women are constructed': the way that 'we are forced to supply the femininity "behind" the photos through *recognition* is part of their power in showing how an ideology works – not by undoing it, but by *doing* it.'

In a more familiar way, conventional fashion photography's representation of women will 'do' ideology rather than 'undo' it – and here too one supplies the femininity through recognition. Fashion photography, of course, has neither the desire nor the capacity to sustain so radical an enquiry into its own codes as Sherman's. Nevertheless, as images of 'woman', fashion photographs are pitted with the recesses, the gaps within and around which Sherman constructs her own (critical) femininity.

This image presents the model as at once object and conflicted subject. The image is thus unbalanced, fissured, capable of being used in a private, possibly deviant, reading of its representation of femininity.

THE REFLEXIVE IMAGE
(Ellen von Unwerth, Plate 27)

Plate 27, a picture of an androgynous beauty sitting up in bed, juxtaposes luxury and disorder. The connection between this disorder and the eroticism of the picture is telling in the highly stylized world of the fashion magazine. The controlled artificiality of the more conventional photograph is the counterpart of this one. Unusually for a fashion photograph the format is a portrait, a 'head shot' which shows no clothes. The model wears only her jewellery in bed. The jewellery is by Chanel, the year 1985, the title of the spread 'Hooked on Classics'. Marilyn Monroe, when asked what she wore in bed, replied 'Chanel No. 5'. The genre is that of the unwitting seductress, a Bardot-like child of nature who appears to defy her status as cultural construct and icon and to reassert her elemental flesh, her warmth.[4] Yet the image is not salacious but intimate.

In its erotic intimacy the picture defines itself against the distancing

27. The reflexive image. Photograph by Ellen Von Unwerth from *The Face*, 66, October 1985. Jewellery by Chanel

objectification of much fashion photography without suggesting the availability of the pornographic image. The nearness of the model and her direct gaze suggest a relationship which in its closeness becomes confounded with a mirror image. The look – ours, hers – is one of recognition. The image captures a gaze that is languid, unguarded, unselfconscious. For women dressing is often about composing an appearance; it can amount to constructing a defence. Fashion imagery, specifically, may construct aloofness, or inviolability. In evoking the moments after waking, the image in Plate 27 gestures towards a time before dressing, before fashion. The photograph is taken before she looks in the mirror, composes herself, and sees herself being seen. The direct gaze of the model makes possible a symbiosis between image and observer, a (perhaps false?) identification of femininity mirrored. The edges of the picture become a mirror frame, the encapsulated image both a possible self and a desirable other. Perhaps the image, functioning as a mirror, captures the moment before one recognizes oneself in it.

In the mirror identity is formed. Plate 27 constructs the model, metaphorically speaking, just prior to her recognizing herself in the mirror, an eye innocent because unseeing, the moment of waking before her image of herself takes command. As spectator one may construct her in a mythical limbo of unselfconsciousness, a Garden of Eden before the Fall, and identify narcissistically with that early state of grace. Narcissism, the love of one's own image, has come to be identified with women. The mirror is traditionally a symbol of female vanity. However, in some psychoanalytic theory the process of mirroring is used as a metaphor for the formation of identity. Reapproaching the mirror from this perspective, it could be argued that the narcissism bound up with looking at fashion images involves a degree of sophistication which exceeds that of simple vanity. Looking at fashion images might involve a continuous redefinition of the self which challenges the idea of a unified subject, as it both makes and unmakes feminine identity.

The model in this picture is both separate, as image, as perfection, and not separate: close, warm, tousled and imperfect. The picture offers the possibility both of narcissistic identification with the perfect 'other' and with the woman before she knows she is a woman, before she makes herself in her own image. There is a phrase, 'putting one's face on', which means putting make-up on, and which designates that ritual before the mirror in which the public face is put on, the sense of self-before-the-world substantiated. It is in this context of relentless awareness of self, that this picture takes on new meanings. Curiously, it connotes a limbo of feminine unself-consciousness, a world miraculously free from the relentless sense of self that women have, of never being able to forget themselves, or how others see them, of endless scrutiny. The model relaxes, invites the spectator to relax, back into the pre-mirror stage of sleepiness and warmth.

Yet this is representation, a portrait as well as a reflection. Might the spectator's pleasure lie simultaneously in the 'consumption' of her beauty, both boyish and voluptuous, and in an identification with her unself-consciousness, which is equally desirable? Like the model in Plate 28 (by the same photographer) she invites a number of fantasies, identifications and responses from the woman spectator. She waits, cigarette poised.

Considering the possibilities of identification and/or objectification which the image seems to offer, is it possible to specify how one reads the image in terms of gender? Does it point to a distinction between a male and a female gaze? Studies in representation have identified, particularly in relation to cinema, a male gaze that is active, voyeuristic and controlling. How do women look? Laura Mulvey describes the 'masculinization' of spectatorship within which 'trans-sex identification' is a habit that very easily becomes, for women, second nature. 'However, this Nature does not sit easily and shifts restlessly in its borrowed transvestite clothes' (Mulvey, 1981, p. 13).

> The transvestite wears clothes which signify a different sexuality, a sexuality which, for the woman, allows a mastery over image and the very possibility of attaching the gaze to desire. Clothes make the man, as they say. Perhaps this explains the ease with which women can slip into male clothing. As both Freud and Cixous point out, the woman seems to be *more* bisexual than the man . . . while the male is locked into sexual identity, the female can at least pretend that she is other – in fact, sexual mobility would seem to be a distinguishing feature of femininity in its cultural construction.
>
> (Doane, 1982, p. 81)

Do women assume a transvestite gaze in relation to images of women which are eroticized, by looking 'as men', with a voyeuristic or controlling gaze? Or is the female gaze narcissistic, one which identifies with the image through likeness and recognition? Perhaps women vacillate between both ways of looking, moving to and fro between two types of gaze as one does with Gombrich's duck/rabbit, an ambiguous drawing which is both a duck and a rabbit (Gombrich, 1960, p. 6). The gaze shifts, alternately constructing the image as either duck or rabbit but never, as Gombrich points out, as both simultaneously.

Perhaps this picture, this fiction, of a half-awake, androgynous model permits both a gaze that is reflexive, narcissistic, mirroring, and a gaze that is 'transvestite', active and masculine. Her half-awakeness positions her between consciousness and unconsciousness, between activity and passivity. It allows the possibility of an indeterminate or bisexual desire, that is, of a visual bisexuality that is, perhaps, part of the way women look at fashion photographs.

THE DISAPPEARING WOMAN
(Ellen von Unwerth, Plate 28)

Plate 28 comes from a six-page fashion spread entitled 'Solitaire'. A series of images shows the same model wandering alone around Paris. The whole feature makes an appeal to a poetic reading, not least in the handwritten 'extracts' from a pseudo-existentialist diary or novel which is intercut with the images and fashion information. In its indeterminacy the image is particularly evocative. Overexposure leaves only a vestigial autumn embankment and a receding figure in a dress blown against her body by the wind. It is a photograph of a woman walking; the modelling of dress and hat appears incidental, although it is of course the *raison-d'être* of the image.

The magazine feature presents a bohemian Paris of secret assignations and poetic loneliness. The dress and large hat suggest an earlier and more romantic epoch, a literary Paris of Baudelaire or Colette. Fashion photographers often strive for a poetic quality, by no means unsuccessfully, as in, for example, Deborah Turbeville's work. When they do succeed it is because of, rather than despite, the limitations of the fashion photograph. Its poetic qualities are a function of the difficulties photographers face in showing something 'more' than clothes. In going beyond the function of showing clothes, fashion photography generates an image that is excessive. Showing the clothes but suggesting something else, something more, the fashion image can be an erotic image in that 'The erotic photograph . . . takes the spectator outside its frame, and it is there that I animate it and it animates me . . . as if the image launched desire beyond what it permits us to see' (Barthes,

28. The disappearing woman. Photograph by Ellen Von Unwerth from *Honey* magazine, March 1986. Clothes by Nigel Preston and the Hat Shop

1984, p. 59). Certainly the suggestion of a spurious 'elsewhere' (in which to wear the clothes) is a selling strategy but it is also something more than that.

As an erotic photograph in this sense, the image here suggests an undefined potential: its meanings float, avoiding a final reading. The lack of fixity or resolution in fashion images is often the quality which holds the spectator's gaze, a precise measure of success in this genre. The fashion image hovers between being a vehicle for fantasy and being insufficient as the *'mise-en-scène* of desire' (Burgin, 1986, p. 98). This failure, institutionalized in the fashion shot, can, as in this image of a disappearing woman, be expressive. The fashion magazine gives a vital context to the transitory image; the poverty of its meanings can become meaningful. Being essentially the photograph of an action — walking — the image (almost) constructs an active subject. Showing her walking away, it underplays the objectification of the model, of women, that is so often a feature of the fashion photograph. In addition the spectator never sees her face, an absence which discourages straightforward identification and encourages a freer kind of association. What is outside the frame is the other point of view, the point of view which would reveal her face. Desiring subject? Desired object? Either way she is disappearing.

In Baudelaire's poem of desire in the street, 'A Une Passante', the poet falls in love with a passer-by, a woman he has never seen before and will never see again. It is because she disappears that she is (potentially) the love of his life: *O toi que j'eusse aimée, toi qui le savais*! ('You whom I might have loved, you who knew it!'). Walter Benjamin observes how, in the sonnet, 'love itself is recognized as being stigmatized by the big city'. This recognition makes the poem a kind of touchstone for the understanding of desire in the modern era: its celebration of 'love at last sight', the recognition that desire is born in loss (Benjamin, 1976, p. 45).

There is a piquant genre of fashion photography which shows the model often at a distance, moving through the city. As in Baudelaire's poem she is 'fugitive', glimpsed. The object of desire cannot be pinned down. The female body in movement, in passing, has a role in generating the euphoria that is a part of the way in which the fashion magazine constructs the 'world' of fashion. But this movement has other meanings, as in this shot of transitory femininity. In its evanescence, its insubstantiality, the fashion image can unhinge our point of view. Where does the woman viewer stand in relation to such images of women?

The voluptuous sinuosity of the figure may attract one without immediately suggesting a sexual identity for the spectator. Just looking, just speculating, one can 'become' this woman who walks away and attract oneself or

106

attract another's gaze. Within the narrative structures of the image (a Parisian scenario) one can identify with the figure as desiring subject; is she hurrying to some secret assignation, or away from one? Is she coming or going? It depends on your point of view and this point of view may be unfixed, multiple and changing. Even this seems too determinate, but it is thus that 'I animate the photograph and it animates me' (Barthes, 1984, p. 59).

In some sense, however, this is an erotic photograph because it launches but cannot sustain desire. Perusing fashion photography one turns the page because one can get nothing more from it. The image is not constructed to satisfy a hunger but to articulate one. Fashion imagery generates images of women for women that both evoke depth and deny meaning. Does the way in which one 'animates' these images characterize a specifically female desire? In being unable to fulfil its promises, the fashion image replicates an absence or a loss, and points towards whatever it is that one doesn't have or can't get, towards desire itself.

FOOTNOTES

1. For example: Veblen, 1953; Flügel, 1930; König, 1973; Barthes, 1985.
2. See, for example: Brooks, 1980; Myers, 1982a; Myers, 1982b; Carter 1982; Shottenkirk, 1983.
3. Charles Jencks, writing about postmodernism and architecture, uses the term 'double-coding' to describe a style or a building which has two independent languages, each with its own audience and integrity, and which is therefore both élitist and populist simultaneously (Jencks, 1984, p. 6).
4. See de Beauvoir, 1980, for a discussion of the phenomenon.

6. DESIGNING WOMEN: THREE COUTURIÈRES

Madeleine Vionnet, Coco Chanel and Elsa Schiaparelli all worked in Paris in the 1920s and 1930s in the exclusive world of *couture*. The contemporary designers discussed in the next chapter, Vivienne Westwood and Rei Kawakubo of Comme des Garçons, an English and a Japanese woman respectively, work in the increasingly international market of ready-to-wear high fashion.

The work of all three *couturières* broke new ground in the meanings which could be made with women's dress. These meanings are not merely of historical interest, although they occurred within the context of the increased mobility of women in the twentieth century; they relate to culturally determined ideas about the female body which are still current. Vionnet, Chanel and Schiaparelli feature in almost all the histories of twentieth-century fashion as established 'stars'. Westwood and Kawakubo await a comparable canonization, although the work of both is in the costume collection of the Victoria and Albert Museum in London, and Kawakubo has already been the subject of a major exhibition at the Fashion Institute of Technology in New York.[1] These two contemporary designers, working in a very different context from the *couturières*, also elaborate, in radical and innovative designs, concerns which relate to the status and meanings which can be ascribed to the female body in contemporary culture. The work of the three *couturières* offers a comparison of approaches to design and fashion, a different angle on the 'woman question' of the early twentieth century. The discussion of their work forms the basis from which to discuss similarities and differences in the approach of two women designers working in a contemporary context.

These five treatments differ somewhat from each other. Differences of approach are, however, determined by differences in the work. Each designer has different concerns; each articulates the female body in different ways and those meanings come to rest in different cultural contexts. This appreciation inevitably raises the question of an adequate methodology with which to discuss fashion design. Fashion history, when it deals with twentieth-century fashion, lacks a discourse in which formal and aesthetic considerations are integrated with social, historical or cultural considerations. It has yet to develop a critical methodology of its own, comparable, for example, to film studies or art history.

The discussion of women's fashion has tended to reproduce unthinkingly preconceptions about femininity. It is clear, however, that the cultural conception of the feminine is capable of being both reproduced and changed in dress. By focusing on the terms of sexual difference, in relation to dress and the body, it may be possible to assess more accurately the ways in which the work itself actively negotiates difference and generates meaning. The rhetoric of fashion which reproduces 'woman' tends to be absent from the work of these five designers. Rather than a single ideal of perfection, their work shows a concern with the multiple refractions of the body in culture. The traditional image of the female body becomes splintered and deflected, resulting in new and challenging 'versions' of the female body and its relative power, definition or drama.

Are there discernible differences in the approach to the female body by women and men designers? Perhaps the answer is not necessarily, or not always. But the work of these five designers, for all its differences, uniformly manifests a concern with the dignity of the body which is worked *with* rather than against. By dealing directly with the body, rather than through the intercession of an idea of 'femininity', they by-pass the dangers of objectification, of discomfort and of traditionalism.

From the late nineteenth century *couture* has been unique in the opportunities it has offered to women for material and critical success. As a professional and creative practice it provided opportunities to women which were denied them in fine art, in painting, sculpture and architecture. In the first two decades of the twentieth century there were slightly more women than men *couturiers*. Their contributions helped to sustain the industries of textiles,

110

embroidery, button-making and accessories. *Couture* enabled them to be both creative designers and businesswomen. In the early years of this century the only comparable area of opportunity was showbusiness, with the difference that the stage requires the presentation of the woman herself as performer and decorative object, rather than as a power behind the scenes.

Couture is an oasis of relatively permanent value (and of documentation) in the desert of fashion's infidelity, its systematic destruction of its own past. This marks *couture* out as an area from which to develop a critical study of fashion design; this contribution to that study focuses on the woman designer designing for women.

VIONNET: DRESS AND THE BODY

Madeleine Vionnet started her apprenticeship at the age of twelve. She was trained as a dressmaker and then as a *couturière* with Callot Soeurs where she cut *toiles* for Mme Gerber, Callot's principal designer. Then Vionnet designed for Doucet for five years before establishing her own firm in 1912 at the age of thirty-six. She closed down during the First World War and reopened in 1918. The body of work discussed below was done in the 1920s and 1930s; in 1939 she shut her atelier for ever following a dispute with her business partner. Vionnet continued to live in Paris until her death in 1974 when she was in her nineties. Vionnet's design work is innovative yet stands outside the different trajectories of avant-gardism in which Chanel or Schiaparelli might be assessed. Her work falls into two categories: the *tailleurs*, tailored suits and capes for the street, and the *robes du soir* and *robes d'après-midi*, in which the fabric is sculpted and draped on the body. In all her work the body is paramount, but whereas the draped dresses are clearly about the body, the *tailleurs*, problematically, make meanings elliptically around the body, a logical function of their being made for a woman on the street as opposed to a woman in a domestic sphere.

In the 1920s the changing status of women and their increasing mobility and independence were issues that women's fashion had to address. The question was one of how women, in the street or travelling, presented themselves outside the context of the domestic interior. Vionnet responded with day clothes that were essentially discreet without being self-effacing. Discussing the Paris collections for 1924–5, a contemporary journal describes Vionnet's *tailleurs*:

The woman of the world who moves through the streets of Paris or who travels should always be soberly and quite impersonally dressed, reserving the indiscreet graces of the floating dress to the *robe d'après-midi* or *du soir* . . . the coats which seem simple and straight hide great research into cut: for the fabric follows the body with only the help of tucks skilfully distributed in a fine network, constituting yet another precious ornament.[2]

(Clercé, 'Les Collections des grands couturiers pour la saison 1924–1925: Jeanne Lanvin, Paul Poiret, Madeleine Vionnet, Worth et Doucet', *Gazette du Bon Ton*, No. 2 for 1924–5)

Although women in the 1920s were appropriating masculine dress and making it their own (the dinner jacket, trousers, the Eton crop, shingling), Vionnet did not use men's tailoring. Where Chanel borrowed the tailoring of men's clothes Vionnet employed a tailoring that was technically and formally specific to her designs for women. In all her work, the outdoor and indoor garments alike, there is a reluctance to cut into the cloth. Vionnet avoided the cutting that gives definition to the Western male suit. Instead, she sculpted one piece to the body by a network of darts and tucks, conveying a tangible sense of the inviolability of the fabric. The *Gazette du Bon Ton* (No. 6 for 1924–5) describes 'ses tailleurs avec leurs tailles indiquées où la nature commande' ('her suits in which nature determines the cut'). In these suits a woman could be anonymous on the street. It is essential that they are not overtly masculine since this was a form of dress adopted by women in the 1920s precisely to draw attention to themselves. Where Vionnet did use masculine details in her *tailleurs* it was not to subvert meanings but to obfuscate them. The clothes function as camouflage; there is a certain intransigence in their refusal to make meanings, a subdued resistance. The woman marks her presence in public by discreet absence.

Anonymity in dress provides protection, specifically for women on the street. Flügel (1930) writes of the psychologically protective and reassuring meanings of clothes. Vionnet's *tailleurs* and cloaks demonstrate both literally and symbolically a protective function. The cape, which she used again and again, both conceals and succours. Vionnet further combined the capes with the suits in an unusual integration of fitted and draped elements. The irregularities of structure always had an aesthetic and functional logic. Freedom of movement joined with the positive qualities of a lovingly fitted and constructed garment.

112

Fashion in the 1920s represented, firstly, freedom through sport and leisure; contemporary magazines are full of articles on flying, motoring, tennis, skiing, golf, mountaineering. The magazine *Femina* in the 1930s showed society ladies in their aeroplanes and motor cars. Activities which are now merely hearty were then emancipating, exciting and fashionable. The New Woman in her tailor-made at the turn of the century could be said to have made the Great Feminine Renunciation in favour of a more masculine form of dress.

It's useless to tell us customs determine fashions. Nothing could be falser. If one observes things with an attentive eye and a spirit detached from current superstitions, it is visible to the contrary that it is fashions which determine customs. Our example is a sure proof, irrefutable, and nothing will persuade me that skiing and bob-sleighing don't owe their success precisely to the fact that they offer women a magnificent opportunity to disguise themselves as men.[3]

(Roger Boutet de Monvel, 'Les Masculines', *Gazette du Bon Ton*, No. 4 for 1922)

Secondly, fashion represented a gamut of interrelated meanings which ranged from the type of dress and behaviour typified by the flapper (a fashion for boyish figures, short hair and tubular dress which de-emphasized waist, hips and breasts) to out and out transvestite dressing.

I was not long deluded by those photographs that show me wearing a stiff mannish collar, necktie, short jacket over a straight skirt, a lighted cigarette between two fingers . . . How timid I was at that period when I was trying to look like a boy, and how feminine I was beneath my disguise of cropped hair. 'Who would take us to be women? Why, women.' They alone were not fooled. With such distinguishing marks as pleated shirt front, hard collar, sometimes a waistcoat, and always a silk pocket handkerchief, I frequented a society perishing on the margin of all societies . . . This clique, or sect, claimed the right of 'personal freedom' and equality with homosexuality, that imperturbable establishment. And they scoffed, as if in whispers, at 'Papa' Lépine, the Prefect of Police, who never could take lightly the question of women in men's clothes.

(Colette, 1971, p. 60–1)

Colette was describing the turn of the century but in the 1920s and 1930s this type of dressing remained largely unchanged from the nineteenth-century model which derived from the dandy.

This was undoubtedly a minority cult of capital cities. But the risqué discussion of changing sex roles that was played out in fashion in the 1920s and 1930s was a context from which Vionnet detached herself. Plate 29 shows a Vionnet flying costume which is in many ways of its period yet it avoids the modernist rhetoric of 1920s fashion. 'I never made fashion, I never saw fashion, I don't know what fashion is. I made the clothes I believe in' (Madeleine Vionnet, quoted Penn, 1977, p. 36).

Madeleine Vionnet is above fashion. Not that she is out of fashion, but she announces the fashion of tomorrow. She has resisted the current religion for the ultra-flat woman, for ridiculous silhouettes which escape the laws of three dimensions. Madeleine Vionnet encourages women to take pride in harmonious proportions, of the fine outline of a chest which is firm and not shameful, and of fine shapely legs.[4]

(*Gazette du Bon Ton*, No. 2 for 1924–5)

While women were busy making social meanings with clothes, Vionnet's formal concerns provided an (apparent) ivory tower from which she worked to undo the socially constructed meanings of the female body.

Throughout the 1920s and 1930s Vionnet made dresses which are a series of variations on a theme. They are bias cut, made in heavy fabrics such as *mousseline*, *crêpe romaine* and *crêpe-de-Chine*, a fabric conventionally used as a lining material. They are unlined but strengthened by bands of grosgrain which prevent them from pulling out of shape. Vionnet never drew but designed in three dimensions by draping the fabric on an 80cm-high wooden doll which was turned on a piano stool as she modelled the fabric to it. 'If I had worked from sketches I should have influenced fashion in quite a different way. You don't take the potentialities of a material into consideration when you're dealing with drawings. To do this you must work on a lay figure, and that is what I always did' (Bertin, 1956, p. 172).

Her fabrics were usually plain, although she made a less successful series of flower-printed dresses in the 1930s, and she sometimes made heavily embroidered evening dresses or dresses in which the design was woven into the cloth. She never used padding; in the romantic revival of the late 1930s, when women took to

114

.THAYAHT. 22

L'ESSAYAGE A PARIS (Croydon-Bourget)

Costume pour tourisme aérien, de Madeleine Vionnet

Traversée a bord d'un avion de " l'Instone Air Line "

29. Madeleine Vionnet, 1922, *'Costume pour tourisme aérien'*: suit for air travel. From the *Gazette du Bon Ton*, No. 4 for 1922. Photograph courtesy of Henry Sotheran Ltd, London

evening dresses with huge skirts, she achieved the necessary volume through cut, by pleating taffeta, rather than by using a crinoline.

Vionnet instigated the bias cut. When fabric is cut on the diagonal the weight of its fall moulds it to the body. The Handkerchief Dress of 1919–20 (Plate 30) shows her preference, at its most abstract, for using bias-cut geometric shapes to drape the body. Four squares of oyster-white *crêpe romaine* are placed on the bias and sewn together at back, front and sides, leaving points on the outside and forming shoulder straps and handkerchief points at the hem. Vionnet herself said: 'The rectangle of fabric, when it is well chosen, is better for making the human form emerge. The angles form exterior parts which, in falling, rise up upon themselves in tiers and sinuous falls, giving the body an outline of the happiest effect, an accompaniment which is brilliant and rich but without superfluity'[5] (*Gazette du Bon Ton*, No. 2 for 1924–5).

In the Handkerchief Dress, and others constructed on the same principle, bias-cut triangles and rectangles are mitred into dresses which slip over the head and fit the body without having any side or back opening. The bias is used in many ways, to make halter necks, cowl necks, petal skirts or handkerchief dresses. In order to meet the demands of cutting on the bias she had her fabrics woven twice as wide as was then customary.

Other garments, cut closer to the body, are realized by moulding the fabric to the body by a system of graduated lozenges or squares made in tucks rather than by cutting into the fabric. The 1936 black organza cocktail dress (Plate 31) is hand-tucked in a chicken-wire pattern so that the pattern is larger across the shoulders and hips, smaller at the waist. This technique, which defines the body by a reticulated pattern which envelopes it, is used in many other dresses, for example in a dress of 1924 where the bodice is made by overlaying a silver lattice, which also forms shoulder straps, on to the magenta crêpe beneath. As with the *tailleurs*, there appears to be an absolute reluctance to cut into the cloth, as if the requirements of the body are mirrored by the inviolability of the cloth. An equivalence is set up between garment and body in which the integrity of one responds to that of the other.

Here, again, Vionnet displays a certain intransigence, a refusal to make of the body a cultural construct. Cutting up and dividing the body in fashion is a way to fix it in history, locate it in time. Instead of this she follows the body's contours with tucks. Vionnet made all her *toiles* herself and her clothes were so skilfully cut that they were virtually impossible to copy. Often asymmetrical, they were designed

30. Madeleine Vionnet, 1922, 'Handkerchief' dress in white *crêpe romaine* cut on the bias. Photograph by Irving Penn

to show the beauty of the body in motion; she wanted 'to dress a body . . . not to construct a dress' (Madeleine Vionnet, quoted Carter, 1977, p. 45). Always the body is paramount. She eliminated interfacings and used lingerie techniques – pin tucking, fagoting, rolled hems – to keep the fabric pliant, in a continual relation to the body. She admired the dancer Isadora Duncan. In an interview in 1954, when Vionnet was seventy-nine, she said: 'It was I who got rid of corsets. At Doucet's, in 1907, I presented mannequins for the first time with bare feet and sandals, and in their own skins' (Bertin, ibid.).

In 1907 Isadora Duncan performed in Paris in a classical tunic which she wore without a corset and with bare legs and sandals. (At this time bare legs broke many more taboos than the *décolletage*.) At the age of ninety-six, in 1973, Vionnet said: 'I have never been able to tolerate corsets myself. So why should I inflict them on other women. *Le corset, c'est une chose orthopédique . . .*' (*The Sunday Times Colour Supplement*, 4 March 1973).

Conventional underwear could not have been worn under Vionnet's bias-cut dresses, some of which have specially made underwear to go with them, also cut on the bias and with seams which corresponded to those on the dress so they did not show through the fabric.

Poiret is usually credited with getting rid of the corset, and Vionnet may have been irritated at never having received the credit for this innovation, made while she was still working for the *couturier* Doucet and before she even set up on her own. Neither of them was strictly the first: in the nineteenth century the Aesthetic Movement and the Society for Rational Dress opposed it; in Vienna as early as 1902 Klimt was designing soft, flowing, uncorseted dresses for the Flöge sisters' fashion house; in Venice in 1907 Fortuny produced his first Delphos dress. Vionnet's uncorseted and draped dresses are consciously classical and timeless. Her perception of the beauty of the female form in movement was radical, with its stress on the natural beauty of the body in contradistinction to the swan-shaped, heavily boned and corseted female silhouette of the turn of the century, the figure described by Poiret as 'a decorated bundle' and earlier by Veblen as 'a monument of conspicuous consumption' (quoted Ginsberg, 1975, p. 11). Her dresses represent not so much a return to nature as an attempt to re-confront the raw material out of which women are (culturally) constructed, actively to mediate between nature and culture via the body and clothing. They are a brave attempt to underdetermine the female body.

Vionnet's dresses were fitted to the body rather than to a corset. The first nipple to appear in *Vogue*, in 1932, can be seen through some Vionnet lingerie, and

31. Madeleine Vionnet, 1936, black silk organza cocktail dress, hand-tucked in a pattern of graduated lozenges. Photograph by Irving Penn

many of the bias-cut dresses of the 1930s were modelled without a brassière. From the beginning of the century she had been designing dresses for *déshabillé* and she clearly intended women to adopt this style in public too, albeit only in the evening dresses. Clearly these clothes are supremely comfortable but only in the literal sense. 'Old sartorial difficulties – trains and whalebone – were exchanged for new ones: the psychologically taxing problems of looking comfortable and dressing simply while being rather exposed. Bad legs or a bad figure had no hiding place, and the need for a good one was never more obvious. Comfort . . . in clothing is a mental rather than a physical condition' (Hollander, 1980, p. 339).

In opposition to the covering, anonymous qualities of her daytime wear, Vionnet's evening dress revealed the body, rather than exposing it. This difference is one of the achievements of her work. Although to be at her ease in a dress by Vionnet a woman had to be comfortable with her own body, her clothes are not designed to challenge the body but, in her own words, to 'accompany' it. However, Vionnet personally was autocratic and refused to dress small dumpy women like herself; there is a comparable autocracy in the clothes, which only look well on beautiful bodies.

Vionnet's bias-cut dresses are the prototype of the satin dresses worn by the Hollywood sex symbols of the 1930s. Although she was recruited to Hollywood, Vionnet never designed successfully there. There is a difference of tone: her work is always underplayed, not for swaggering or showing off. Jean Harlow was often dressed by Adrian, a Hollywood designer who, while adopting the type, never produced either the sophistication or the subtlety of Vionnet's cut. Her single-minded dedication to cut and construction, which eliminates extraneous fastening and decoration, leads to a purity which is proto-minimalist.[6] Where Hollywood constructed the female body as spectacle, Vionnet works in the opposite direction. Paradoxically the primacy of the body guarantees it a kind of discretion or anonymity.

Nevertheless, Jean Harlow displayed in Vionnet-inspired dresses by Adrian inevitably modifies any reading of Vionnet's clinging dresses as simply freeing the female form. There is in Vionnet's work a polemical tension between the body and the dress which was always linked to its period, despite the ahistoricism of her clothes. Plate 32 shows a detail from an evening dress of the mid 1930s. The fabric wraps the body like a black bandage. On the bottom, where one might expect a bow, a signifier of jovial sauciness, the black silk taffeta is instead extruded and twisted into a knot which resembles nothing so much as a tourniquet.

32. Madeleine Vionnet, 1934–5. Detail of an evening dress in which the black silk taffeta is twisted and knotted at the back. Photograph by Irving Penn

CHANEL: THE NEW WOMAN AS DANDY

Chanel – above all else, is a style.

(Coco Chanel, quoted Charles-Roux, 1981, p. 244)

Chanel's contribution to women's fashion was the adaption of the forms and details, but above all the meanings, of a certain type of masculine dress to that of women. In doing so she developed a style which seemed, particularly at the height of her influence in the 1920s, to express the aspirations of early twentieth-century women towards independence and mobility. Here the implications of her use of masculine dress and her approach to style are discussed in relation to the idea of dandyism, that essentially masculine cult of distinction and ascendancy which is crucially mediated through style and dress. Additionally, her work is considered within the context of the rigours of modernist design.

Chanel began her career in the fashionable world as a mistress. Using her talents as a milliner she opened her first shop in 1913 with the financial backing of her protector.[7] For Chanel, in whom the ambition of the *demi-mondaine* was coupled with the New Woman's desire for status, the conventions of the upper-class male wardrobe represented both power and independence. However, Chanel came from an obscure provincial background and was not the type of middle-class New Woman who was a feminist. There is a photograph of her in 1910 at the races, a parading ground for high fashion at the time, wearing a tie and a man's coat – too big in the shoulders, too long in the sleeves (Charles-Roux, ibid.). Chanel likened women's presence at the races during this era to that of medieval women at a tournament (ibid., p. 83). She herself, whose presence there was circumscribed by her position as a mistress, nevertheless may be seen to assert her self-determination through wearing the clothes of her male protector.

In the late eighteenth and early nineteenth century George Brummell, the prototype of the dandy, made upper-class English country clothes, especially riding clothes, into the height of men's fashion in the city. In the early 1800s the alterations he made, particularly with regard to fit and cut, established these as the critical signifiers in men's dress. Brummell's style, particularly for day, was essentially restrained and disciplined, and set a standard of sober discretion, appropriateness and taste which governed men's clothing until well into the twentieth century. The style was at once élitist and democratic: democratic because it was relatively 'ordinary' and élitist because very few men could get it right – that depended on the coexistence of money, leisure and, the odd one out, skill. All this in Brummell went with a relentless superficiality with regard to the serious things in life and spectacular social climbing. Brummell's kind of dandyism instigated 'the idea of establishing a new kind of aristocracy, an aristocracy based on talent' (Baudelaire, 1981, p. 421). Over the years this kind of cultural and social *coup* has been played out in different ways but has remained, like the twentieth-century concept of the avant-garde, a fundamentally male preserve.

Dandyism offers the possibility of social mobility on one's own, albeit restricted, terms. Within dandyism the whole idea of social marginality becomes dynamic. But the marginalization of women cuts across class and excludes the deliberate play on social marginality which dandyism offers. Furthermore, dandyism flirts with the conventionally feminine areas of narcissism, artificiality and fashion. The dandy demonstrates his control by the way in which he survives trivialization, the way in which he is not emasculated by it. For women, the construction of femininity prescribes triviality, making it less easy to flirt with.

Increasingly, however, dandyism in both Britain and France became an area in which men questioned the conventions of mid-nineteenth-century masculinity. In *The Dandy: from Brummell to Beerbohm*, Ellen Moers stresses the importance of the fusion of masculine and feminine elements in the Second Empire dandy and comments: 'For the *fin-de-siècle*, the nature of the gentleman was a minor question. Wilde's era asked, with a new urgency, what is meant merely to be a man' (Moers, 1960, p. 308). Moers goes on to argue that the New Woman, who was ambitious and determined to win her independence, pushed the *fin-de-siècle* dandy from the centre stage. The nineteenth-century ideal of masculine power based on moral strength and energy had been eroded and was subsequently denounced by the avant-garde of the 1890s. This left a space for the pragmatic, upwardly mobile New Woman of which Chanel is in certain ways an excellent example, in spite of her early career as a music-hall singer and kept woman. One could argue that the spirit in which the so-called New Woman took up the values of purpose and ambition, of self-control, inflexibility and even respectability, and her espousal of the rigidities of the male wardrobe (shirts, ties and the 'tailor-made' suit), were entirely reactionary were it not for the progressive politics of women's emancipation that went with them.

It was the identification with women's emancipation which gave such an anti-decorative uniform its appeal to women. In the hands of Chanel the look was also glamorous. In borrowing from the male wardrobe Chanel drew on the way in which men's clothes, within the terms of classical male dandyism, could signify personal independence within a rigid order. Dandyism established for men's clothes a coherent scale of distinctions and a precise language of social hierarchy. The association of women's clothes with feminine beauty and attraction tends to privilege aesthetic meanings over social ones. Dandyism fused the social and the aesthetic in men's dress, and gave form to an ambivalence in the relation of the individual to the social world, one of belonging and not belonging, of conformity and rebellion. Dandyism made possible a kind of *incognito*, an unmistakable yet understated disguise: the possibility of not being what you seem. Returning to the photograph of Chanel at the races, a mistress has a 'uniform', she is supposed to look the part, well dressed yet not aspiring to total respectability and, it goes without saying, feminine. The status of the successful *fin-de-siècle* courtesan was distinct from that of both the aristocratic and the bourgeoise woman and carried a corresponding power in matters of dress. By contrast Chanel looks sporting, tasteful and energetic, with that added touch of personal style, almost of insolence – the man's coat and tie – which calls her status into question and yet gives nothing away. Charles-Roux suggests that she stripped her wardrobe of adornment to avoid the reputation of the kept woman (ibid., p. 51). If dandyism is about hiding things, Chanel, by all accounts, felt she had much to hide.

Gabrielle Chanel, whose social position as a young woman was both created and stigmatized by being a mistress, belonged in her youth to the *demi-monde*. She had every reason to want to alter the rules of a social order in which, for example, it was unusual for a dress-maker or *couturière* to mix socially with her clients.

The fact that the *demi-monde* is so frequently a pioneer in matters of fashion is due to its peculiarly uprooted form of life. The pariah existence to which society condemns the *demi-monde* produces an open or latent hatred against everything that has the sanction of the law, of every permanent institution, a hatred that finds its relatively most innocent and aesthetic manifestation in striving for ever new forms of appearance. In this continual striving . . . there lurks an aesthetic expression of the desire for destruction.

(George Simmel quoted in Wilson, 1985, p. 138)

With reference to Chanel herself Paul Morand spoke of 'that advanced guard of country girls . . . who go out, confront the dangers of the city, and triumph, doing so with that solid appetite for vengeance that revolutions are made of' (quoted in Charles-Roux, ibid., p. 61). Chanel's defiance of the social restrictions imposed on her by her sex and class underlie the style for which she became famous. A significant part of that style was her dislike of women's clothes as jokes or entertainment, and her insistence on a dignity that was invulnerable. Poiret paid her a back-handed compliment when he accused her of '*de luxe* poverty' ('*miserabilisme de luxe*': Charles-Roux, ibid., p. 157). Chanel spoke fiercely about the display of riches, reserving a special disgust for women who publicly show off priceless jewels – she described it as 'obscene'. This seemingly envious rage became sublimated in one of the cornerstones of the Chanel style, masses of fake jewellery. She is reputed to have reassured her richest clients that it was all right to wear their real jewels so long as they looked fake.

If the radicalism that is associated with Chanel as a designer can be understood in terms of the 'solid appetite for vengeance' of the *demi-mondaine*, it was also supported by the rejection of sentiment and nostalgia which characterized the early years of modernism. Within this context, Chanel's innovations of simplicity, severity and outdoorsiness gather new meanings.

In 1913 there was no sports fashion as such for women and Chanel's sporting inclinations prompted her to design clothes for her own outdoor pursuits. In the 1920s she was to be much influenced by Suzanne Lenglen, a tennis champion with a distinctive and idiosyncratic style in dress. Many of the clothes Chanel borrowed from the male wardrobe were sporting clothes; men's sporting clothes were created for the leisure activities of the upper class and Chanel, like Brummell before her, saw the potential both of their genuine practical value and of their aristocratic associations. Sport, 'whenever it is a signified in fashion . . . achieves a luxury form of doing, a useless transitivity, it is both active and idle' (Barthes, 1985, p. 250). Men's sporting wear had long incorporated elements of working-class dress in the interests of ease of movement, durability and, perhaps, of the assertion of a more 'elemental' masculinity. As early as 1913 Chanel made beach wear for herself out of *tricot*, or jersey, a soft, flexible material then considered suitable only for underwear. The early *tricot* sport suits were of simple untailored construction, with patch pockets and a version of the sailor collar, all elements which derived from men's work clothes. When she opened her first dress shop in 1914 these suits in silk or wool jersey were among her first successes.

Plate 33 shows a summer coat of 1918 in black satin, lined and trimmed with black and white tartan. The coat bears interesting similarities to the suit of 1959 in Plate 37. The satin coat and the hat exemplify the influential combination of an almost modest lack of ostentation or ceremony with a boyish and sporting dash. Plate 34 shows a motoring coat of 1919, an item of sportswear which is made up in dark blue *tricot*. The use of this soft and flexible material is combined with the austerity and lack of adornment characteristic of the male wardrobe as handed down by Brummell.

Later Chanel was at the forefront of that reversal of the aesthetic of centuries which made the tan fashionable, in keeping with the atavistic modernism of the 1920s. One might speculate that for Chanel personally such reversals were a gratifying expression of her power to lead the *beau monde*. It should also be noted that the tan was particularly taboo for women, especially for women who had any pretension to being 'a lady', so that here was an aesthetic initiative in keeping with Chanel's social motivations. The central, radical thrust of her work in the 1920s was informed by the attack on individual social restrictions in the interest of self-advancement. Hers is the modernism of the woman careerist. Despite her reputation for chic, Chanel was essentially unsophisticated, hard-headed and ruthless. She was a primitive in the artistic circles in which she moved; Colette described her as 'a little black bull' (Charles-Roux, ibid., p. 182). Popular modernism in the 1920s demanded figures of the kind of toughness that Chanel embodied.

Chanel's early work exemplifies the modernist project in design to dispense with superfluous detail and decoration, and to espouse the cause of functionalism. This is already evident in her sportswear (Plates 33 and 34) and becomes institutionalized in the little black dress (Plate 35). American *Vogue* predicted in 1926 that the little black dress of the 1920s would become a sort of uniform and concluded, 'Here is a Ford signed "Chanel"' (quoted in Charles-Roux, ibid., p. 156). More generally, the functionalist or anti-decorative move in art and design may indicate a rejection of the feminine in favour of an exclusively masculine model of power. In this context Chanel's dandyism and her modernism are interlocked.[8] Plate 36 shows a black, sequinned cardigan evening suit worn with a sleeveless jersey top. The anti-decorative rhetoric of Chanel's modernist approach is maintained here despite the abundant use of sequins. The machine aesthetic is exemplified by the suit's metallic sheen, straight lines and tubular forms.

The changes in women's fashion represented by Chanel's early work of 1914–20 were preceded by the changes associated with the work of the designer Paul

CHANEL

33. Chanel, 1918. Black satin summer coat edged and lined with black and white tartan. From British *Vogue*, July 1981. © The Condé Nast Publications Ltd

Poiret. In 1907 Poiret, like Vionnet, was designing clothes which dispensed with the nineteenth-century corset. A brilliant publicist, Poiret's attack on the corset succeeded where others had failed. Dress reform movements and the Aesthetic Movement had challenged the popularity of the corset; Poiret made its removal fashionable by transforming all the other features of women's dress at the same time, producing a completely new aesthetic. Inspired by the East and coming to prominence at the same time as the Russian Ballet, Poiret's work was associated with a new, and possibly subversive, eroticism.[9] It combined violent colour with delicacy, eroticism with playfulness, exoticism with a light touch. This work successfully countermanded the prevailing fashions of the time and soon made the statuesque and upholstered woman of the *belle époque* a thing of the past.

Poiret's feminine ideal was a decorative and beguiling *odalisque*, her non-conformism signified by her identification with sensuousness and pleasure. The Poiret woman moved in an interior world, a seductive 'elsewhere'. By contrast the woman Chanel designed for belonged in an exterior world, a world of an increasingly streamlined modernism. She was anti-decorative and active. The modernist aesthetic of the woman in motion replaced 'being' with 'doing'. Everything that Poiret stood for as a designer was anathema to Chanel, who always spoke of 'going out' when she spoke of fashion: 'If . . . there are no more *robes d'intérieur* . . . it is undoubtedly because there are no more interiors' (Chanel, quoted in Charles-Roux, ibid., p. 138), and, 'Fashion does not exist unless it goes down into the streets. The fashion that remains in the salons has no more significance than a costume ball' (ibid., p. 237).

The two great male designers with whom Chanel may be seen to contend in her career – Poiret in the 1900s and Dior in the 1950s – shared a feeling for women as the purveyors of domestic charm and decorativeness. This contrasts sharply with the briskness of Chanel's approach and her almost misogynistic rejection of the idea of femininity that is implicit in Poiret's work. While it was Chanel's approach which became associated with the progress of women's emancipation in the early twentieth century there is a very different conception of liberation in women's fashion held out in the kind of avant-gardism of Poiret. The latter would require a re-evaluation of the idea of femininity, the former its rejection in favour of the emulation of a masculine model of power and effectiveness. At the time the First World War determined the issue: Chanel won. Her crisp, unexpansive style dominated the 1920s. A woman in a little black dress or suit with very short hair, a cloche hat and a cigarette became the compelling figure in fashion (see Plate 35).

34. Chanel, 1919. Motor coat in dark
blue *tricot*. From British *Vogue*, August
1919. © The Condé Nast Publications
Ltd

Poiret was to lament the end of an era when he said: 'Formerly women were architectural, like the prows of ships, and very beautiful. Now they resemble little undernourished telephone clerks' (quoted in Charles-Roux, ibid., p. 157). Clearly the telephone-clerk look had its glamour in the 1920s; the style of Chanel was about doing things rather than being things. Needless to say the telephone clerk or secretary could not afford Chanel but the style was relatively easy to imitate. Like Brummell, Chanel in the 1920s and 1930s promoted a style that in many ways traded on its 'ordinariness' but was one which she had the satisfaction of knowing very few women could get right.

In the 1950s Chanel made a comeback in her seventies with the clothing that she is best known for, the 'Chanel suit'. Her comeback followed a period of exile after her association with a high-ranking German officer during the occupation of Paris in World War II. She was reactionary politically and a feature of all her activities was her love of power and her contempt for the side which was not winning. She paid for her collaboration during the German occupation, though less dearly than some, in being obliged, after the liberation in 1944, to retire to Switzerland, where she remained for the next eight years.

In 1947 Christian Dior's New Look triumphed in Paris and when Chanel entered the arena again in 1954 it was with typical competitiveness to take on the talent of designers like Dior, Balenciaga and Fath, whom she referred to as 'ces messieurs' (ibid., p. 235). Referring to Dior's New Look she said: 'Was he mad, this man? Was he making fun of women? How, dressed in "that thing", could they come and go, live or anything?' (ibid., p. 204).

Chanel asserted her right to dress women over that of any man: 'men were not meant to dress women' (ibid., p. 235). Dior's New Look had been a fashion *coup* of the first order which reawoke Europe and America to the power of fashion. It has conventionally been described as a return to a more feminine style after the lack of indulgence and subtlety of wartime fashion and that of the initial recovery period. Elizabeth Wilson, however, argues that the romanticism and nostalgia of the New Look had its roots in the developments of Paris fashion during the Nazi occupation and goes so far as to describe it as 'morbid if not fascist' (Wilson, 1985, pp. 44–6). She writes of the stiffness, spikiness and sharpness of the New Look as 'weirdly masculine'. Perhaps the spikiness of the New Look may be understood in terms of fetishism. Certainly it revelled in its impracticality; perhaps the most indubitably 'feminine' thing about it was that it was restricting, requiring, especially in its *couture* form, a return to waspies and stiff petticoats. Part of Chanel's promotional

35. Chanel, 1926. Little black dress in crepella. From British *Vogue*, October 1926. © The Condé Nast Publications Ltd

gambit for her new designs in 1954 was to pour invective on such designs, their designers, and any woman who would consent to wear them. The work she produced, in contrast, made ease look infinitely better than discomfort. She reworked the day and evening suits which were her staple. The typical Chanel daytime suit of the 1950s and 1960s was in highly textured material, usually knobbly tweed, often in untweedy colours like pink and black, and sometimes with an overlarge check. Again she used elements of the male wardrobe and altered them, re-gendering them. The jacket was worn with a slightly flared, knee-length skirt and was lined in the same material as the short sleeved or sleeveless shirt. This lining would appear at the cuffs and collar of the cardigan jacket in a way that was structurally different from, yet reminiscent of, the look of a man's shirt collar and cuffs when worn with a suit. The whole thing was worn with low heeled shoes. The look was elegant and comfortable, controlled yet casual. Despite its variations, her work of different periods exhibits the same basic concerns. The suit of 1959 shown in Plate 37 retains certain essential characteristics of the coat of 1918 in Plate 33. Chanel's work of the 1950s extended its influence to ready-to-wear fashion when it 'went down into the streets' via young designers like Mary Quant. The simplicity and casualness of the look became the signifiers of youthfulness, a quality which was central to Chanel's approach to women's fashion.

Chanel died in 1971. Her working career spanned half a century, a period which saw significant changes in the position of women. These changes are reflected in a body of work which is closely bound up with the redefinitions of femininity during the modernist period. Chanel is associated with the liberation of women's fashion. The clothes were comfortable and easy to wear in the literal sense, yet their definition and simplicity signified a formal control that derived from a masculine model. Her design practice suggests that, for women, dressing for power involves the adoption of a masculine cult of distinction.[10] At once revolutionary and conservative, Chanel's work constitutes a dialectic on the contradictions within the workings of the feminine will to power as it is played out in patriarchy.

SCHIAPARELLI: A CRISIS IN VOCABULARY[11]

Elsa Schiaparelli was born in 1883, the daughter of an old and distinguished Roman family. As a young woman she moved in intellectual and artistic circles in London,

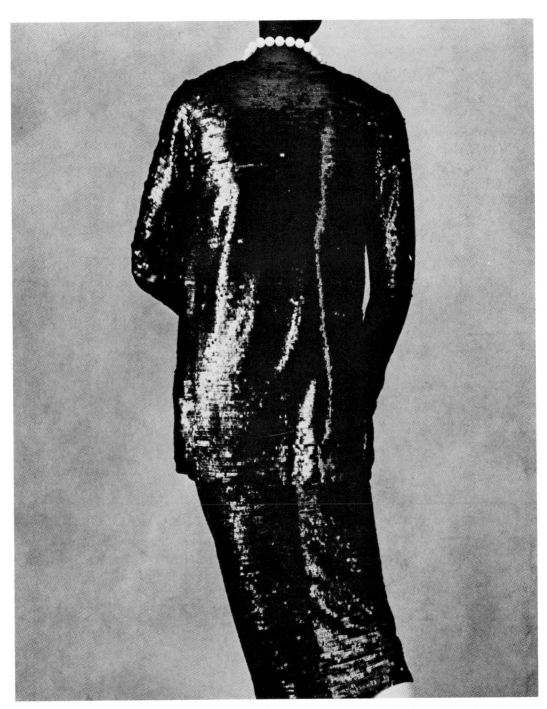

36. Chanel, 1926. Black sequinned evening suit with cardigan jacket and straight skirt worn with a sleeveless jersey top. Photograph by Irving Penn

Paris and New York. She settled in Paris in the 1920s where she came to know Paul Poiret who gave her his designs to wear and encouraged her talents. She came to fashion design by accident with no formal training and was spurred on by economic necessity. Her influence on fashion reached its peak in the mid to late 1930s and the work of that period is the focus of this discussion. During the Second World War she returned to America but reopened her *couture* house in Paris from 1945–54, although without her pre-war success. Schiaparelli died in 1973.

Schiaparelli's work proposes fashion as a discourse of perversity and play. Behind her handling of women's fashion is a meditation on the wider category of dress itself as a cultural language which inscribes the body. Schiaparelli's approach to dress centres around an understanding of how it acts simultaneously to repress the body and to bring it into the realm of language – the symbolic. As repressed material, one might speak of the body as the 'unconscious' of clothing.

Schiaparelli's famous 'jokes', for example the Shoe Hat (Plate 39), are made with reference to this repressed unconscious. Her work shows an acute sensitivity to the displacement that occurs in the relationship of the body to clothes and adornment.[12] This understanding informs the fetishistic play in her work, a play which involves the sense of touch as much as that of sight. If her work is shocking it is in the way she uses displacement to suggest ways in which the irrational is at work and at play within the language of clothes. It is this practice too which links her work in fashion design with that of Surrealism in sculpture, painting and photography.

Her first success, in 1927, was the famous hand-knitted sweater with a *trompe-l'oeil* bow knitted in at the neck. A number of features make this first success exemplary. There is a calculated reversal of fashion codes: a hand-knitted garment gains over the fashionableness of the ultra-modern machine-knitted sweaters pioneered by Chanel (the rivalry of these two was to become legendary in the 1930s). Hand-knitted garments are oddments, or one-offs, which confer a sense of uniqueness. Schiaparelli emphatically opposed snobbery in fashion, or reversed it, here paradoxically by promoting the work of the hand over that of the machine. In an anti-decorative era there is wit in the discovery of illusory decoration and the use of *trompe-l'oeil* is her hallmark, a symptom of her sensitivity to the relation between dress and illusion.

The *garçonne* silhouette which Chanel and Patou had instigated in the 1920s was replaced by Schiaparelli with a silhouette which emphasized padded shoulders and a waist. This new shape, and the wearing of longer skirts, is seen by

37. Chanel, 1959. Cardigan suit in tweed with a black and white check silk lining and shirt. Photograph from British *Vogue*, April 1959, by Henry Clarke. © The Condé Nast Publications Ltd

fashion commentators as a return to a more conventional femininity after the 'novelties' of the 1920s. However, in the hands of Schiaparelli this emphatic yet ambiguous shape is an oddity. It combines masculine and feminine clothing signifiers in such a way that they virtually cancel each other out, leaving an emphasis on shape and the power of fashion to determine it. For all the boxy severity of some of her designs, notably the suits, Schiaparelli's work always foregrounds ornamentation, in trimmings, accessories and the use of colour. In this way, without hampering the wearer, her work eschews an affiliation with the rhetoric of functionalism and simplicity associated with male dress and, in the 1920s, with the ideology of progress in women's fashion. Schiaparelli's preoccupation with dress as costume, or masquerade, and with the ornamental, pivots the meanings of her work around a conception of the feminine, not least when she borrows the features of a guardsman's uniform.

Her work in the 1920s developed the idea of fashion as an assemblage of clothing references. Many of her designs revolve around the 'fashionalization' of symbolic or anti-fashion garments and adornments – a clown's hat, a sailor's tattoo. In pointing to the culturally bizarre or anthropologically curious aspects of adornment (for both sexes) she highlights Western women's fashion as a category of dress no less bizarre and curious, opening it up to speculation. The system of references operates most clearly in her approach to accessories and hats, in which her ostensibly arbitrary and eclectic form of *bricolage* interferes with the designated categories of objects only to make other, less obvious, connections. From countless examples one might pick a black handbag which looked like a telephone, a cap of corrugated velvet which looked like a brain, a necklace made of aspirins (designed for her by Louis Aragon and Elsa Triolet) and buttons which were, in her own words, 'anything but buttons' – peanuts, padlocks, typewriter keys. Functional details in her clothes were turned into curiosities, inviting scrutiny and investigation. Schiaparelli was the first to use zips, formerly concealed, visibly, profusely and provocatively. By playing with objects and their associations she presented garments themselves as objects, the relics or talismans of a strange social ritual – dressing.

Schiaparelli embraced the contingency of fashion and celebrated the transitoriness of its meanings. In her approach there is an implicit recognition that it is the contingency of fashion that lies behind both its low cultural status and its power. Her work is fundamentally anti-élitist and celebratory, it suggests that anyone can play. She counteracted the élitism of *couture* by frequent references to working clothes, be it the circus performer's spangled bolero, the worker's overalls which she brought into fashion as a jumpsuit, or the hats of Danish fisherwomen, made of the first newsprint fabric, printed with articles about herself. Her clothes were expensive but were extensively and cheaply copied. More importantly the approach was, and continues to be, entirely accessible. She pioneered the use of artificial textiles and experimented with materials like rubber and nylon. She made a point of using newly invented textiles which imitated high-status materials like silk and fur. Her interest in deception extended to the use of materials which are unfamiliar, or not what they seem, as, for example, in the 'tree bark' dress, or the transparent 'glass' cape of 1936 made out of 'Colcombet's synthetic rhophane', a kind of cellophane. Her love of novelties, her creation of clothes which are virtually toys, is transformed, in a modern idiom, into a celebration of popular culture within *couture* by contemporary designers such as Vivienne Westwood or Jean Paul Gaultier.

Her use of colour was a further challenge to conventional taste and the restraint practised in Western dress. Her most famous breach was in the deployment of the colour she named 'Shocking Pink' and which she described as 'not [a colour] of the West' (Schiaparelli, 1954, p. 97). Schiaparelli brought off almost any combination of colours with a mastery of tone but ultimately her use of colour was theatrical rather than painterly. For the women who were her clients Schiaparelli's clothes offered the possibility of transgressing standards of good taste and of debunking the codes of decorum in women's fashion. One client recalled: 'For us 'Schiap' was much more than a matter of dresses: through clothes she expressed a defiance of aesthetic conventions in a period when *couture* was in danger of losing itself in anaemic subtleties'[13] (Nadia Georges Picot, quoted Garnier, 1984, p. 125).

Schiaparelli's work draws comparisons with Surrealism and Dada. She knew Picabia and Duchamp in New York; in Paris she involved Cocteau, Dali and Bérard in her work. But rather than using the association with fine art to give status to fashion design, it seems important to understand how Surrealist themes in particular are played out in her work. For all its fundamental radicalism (revolution and psychoanalysis), or perhaps because of it, Surrealism had enormous popular appeal. It permeated fashion in the 1930s, particularly fashion photography.

Within Surrealism, woman was the image and agent of inspiration, her evocation a challenge to the repressive order of logic and commonsense. A central concern with sexuality formed itself around the image of the eroticized female body. At the same time, the feminine was a metaphor for Surrealism's play on appearances, a discourse of illusion, artifice and masquerade. As a fashion designer Schiaparelli was well placed to explore and develop such themes; as a woman designer she turned

38. Schiaparelli, 1937–8. 'Tear' dress and head shawl. The dress is in silk crêpe with a printed *trompe-l'oeil* design of ripped fabric by Salvador Dali. On the shawl the rips are appliquéd flaps of fabric. Photograph by courtesy of the trustees of the Victoria and Albert Museum

this to particular account. In her work the theme of femininity as a form of choreographed deception becomes self-conscious, constructive and critical.

Women artists in Surrealism developed a language of the erotic that used Surrealism's device of displacement in specific ways. It was in terms of an oblique approach to their own sexuality and their own bodies that women artists in Surrealism explored feminine disguise and masquerade.[14] In Schiaparelli's work too there is an avoidance of the obviously sexual and displacement is used to negotiate the sexual meanings of dress, as in a hat with a veil which covers the mouth but leaves the eyes uncovered. Her work suggests the relation of women to their bodies as the baffling one of self-observation. Echoing Breton's description of Picasso's paintings as 'tragic toys for adults' (quoted Hamilton, 1972, p. 391), Schiaparelli's clothes could be described as tragic toys for women.

Schiaparelli's collaborations with Dali are among her most famous pieces. The Tear Dress of 1937–8 (Plate 38) powerfully counterposes violence and anxiety with poise and tranquillity. The print of *trompe-l'oeil* rips for this tight, full-length evening dress was inspired by Dali. It is worn with a separate shawl (worn on the head) which has the same tear motif but in appliquéd organza flaps, carefully stitched to resemble rips. On the dress the 'rips' are gashes of purple and black, the colours of bruised and torn flesh; on the shawl they are pink tongues. The imagery of violence is counterposed by the elegance of the dress, its existence as sophisticated fashion, and the fact that it is *not* rags, *not* torn. The way in which dress acts to displace sexual meanings from the body is brilliantly exploited. It is a piece suggestive of fantasy that is both acknowledged and denied. Violence and eroticism are simultaneously displayed and made to disappear; beauty is brought to bear on rupture.

The other celebrated Dali collaboration was the Shoe Hat of 1937–8. The Shoe Hat was worn with a black cocktail suit in which the edges of the pockets are appliquéd to look like lips (Plate 39). The hat, in the shape of an inverted high-heeled shoe, is shown here in the all-black version; it was also made with a shocking pink heel. Schiaparelli's work is imbued with an appreciation of the fetishistic function of dress.[15] In the Shoe Hat ensemble the associations of pocket/mouth/vagina play against those of hat/high heel/phallus. The piece suggests the body and its relation to clothes as an interface of multiple fetishistic possibilities. Flügel (1930) rests much of his analysis on an understanding of the unconscious displacement of emotion from the body to clothes, in particular the deflection of sexual interest. He further suggests that the best wearer of clothes, the leader of

fashion, will be the man or the woman who effects this displacement most successfully. In Schiaparelli's work there is a remarkable transference of interest from the body on to clothes — it is on clothes, rather than the body, that she paints her images of self-display. As fashion, the ensemble of the Shoe Hat and suit are brilliantly transgressive in their appropriation and further inversion of the perverse meanings of women's dress. As a suggestion of something done (putting a shoe on your head) it evokes the polymorphous perversity of childhood.

Whitney Chadwick comments that women Surrealist painters often used animal imagery in the representation of themselves as 'poised uneasily between the worlds of art and nature' (Chadwick, 1985b, p. 114). Schiaparelli's work is full of animal and natural symbolism. She uses insect motifs, notably in a clear plastic necklace painted with realistic insects which appear to be crawling on the wearer's skin. Using fur, she brought an animal 'otherness' to bear on its usual associations with softness and femininity. In her use of animal imagery and associations she disturbs the familiar discrimination between the natural world and the cultural world of which fashionable dress is the emblem.

In the Lamb Chop Hat the wearer becomes playfully associated with a piece of meat served for consumption. A white ruffle fixes the meaning of the object as food rather than dismembered animal. In ways that are at once disturbing and comical the work plays on an analogy between garnishing food and the use of adornment in women's dress, in which the 'raw' of woman is transformed into the 'cooked' of femininity. Apparently only Schiaparelli herself could be brought to wear the hat. It might be compared to, may even have been inspired by, Meret Oppenheim's 'Ma Gouvernante, Mein Kindermächen, My Nurse' of 1936 in which a pair of high heels, lashed together, are served upside down on a salver with similar ruffles on their heels.[16]

At the heart of Schiaparelli's sense of style is her understanding of clothes as costume, of fashion as performance. Within the theatricality of her work the woman is presented as a performer, a masquerader. She creates herself as spectacle; but the moment she displays herself she also disguises herself. In this way the theme of women's anonymity in the street, in public, takes a new turn. The woman may disguise herself by flaunting herself. Mary Ann Doane points out that 'the masquerade, in flaunting femininity, holds it at a distance' (Doane, 1982, p. 81). By creating herself as spectacle, ironically, as Schiaparelli did, a woman puts a distance between herself and her observers, a space within which to manoeuvre and to determine the meanings of the show. She takes control of the mask, the disguise,

39. Schiaparelli, 1937. Black hat in the form of an inverted high-heeled shoe, worn with a black cocktail suit with pocket edges appliqúed in the shape of lips. Photograph by courtesy of the trustees of the Victoria and Albert Museum

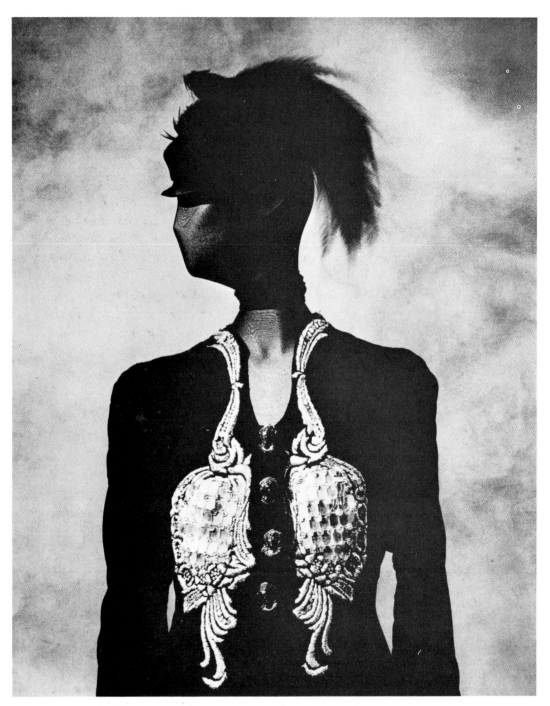

40. Schiaparelli, 1939. Black velvet jacket with upside-down hand mirrors appliqúed with gold tinsel and pieces of real mirrored glass, worn with a long black dinner dress and a plumed cap. Photograph by Irving Penn

that is femininity.

The *Commedia dell'Arte* collection of 1939 featured black tricorne hats worn with masks, making explicit the ludic motif. Her use of themes for each collection, such as the circus, reiterates the underlying concerns in her work with poetic deception, allusion and play. If women are condemned to 'watch themselves being looked at' (Berger, 1972, p. 47), Schiaparelli pursues the problem into the theatre. Plate 40 shows a black velvet jacket worn over a long black dinner dress. The ensemble, with the plumed cap, is from the Music collection of 1937–8. The buttons of the jacket are in the form of sculpted female heads. On the breasts two upside-down hand mirrors are embroidered and appliquéd in gold tinsel and pieces of real mirrored glass. The duplicated symbols of feminine vanity become a warrior's breastplate, armour, military uniform. It is the observer rather than the wearer who is reflected, dazzled. As a rococo anachronism the mirrors evoke a fairytale hall of mirrors. Thus upholstered, clothes become furniture, the body a stage set. The theatricality of Schiaparelli's work proposes the woman as actress, in terms of both tragic irony and comedy. Ultimately her work suggests that the woman must *play* her way out of her predicament, the impasse of femininity.

FOOTNOTES

1. The exhibition showed the work of Madeleine Vionnet, Claire McCardell and Rei Kawakubo. For the catalogue, see Fashion Institute of Technology (1987).
2. 'La femme du monde qui circule par les rues de Paris ou qui voyage, doit toujours être sobrement, assez impersonellement vêtue, réservant les grâces indiscrètes du flou aux robes d'après-midi et du soir . . . Les manteaux à l'aspect simple et droit recèlent de grandes recherches de coupe: car il s'agit pour l'étoffe de suivre le corps à l'aide seulement de "repincés" savamment distribués en fines nervures, qui constituent encore un ornement précieux.'
3. 'Car, n'est-ce pas, inutile de venir nous raconter que les moeurs déterminent les modes. Rien de plus faux. Si l'on observe les choses d'un oeil attentif et l'esprit dégagé des superstitions courantes, il est visible au contraire que ce sont les modes qui font les moeurs. L'example qui nous occupe en est une preuve certaine, irréfutable, et nulle me persuadera que le ski et le bobsleigh ne doivent pas leur succès a ce que précisément ils offrent aux femmes une occasion magnifique de se déguiser en hommes.'
4. 'Madeleine Vionnet est au-dessus de la mode. N'entendez point qu'elle soit hors de la mode, mais bien qu'elle annonce la mode de demain. Elle a résisté à la religion momentanée de la femme ultra-plate, des silhouettes ridicules, qui échappent à la loi des trois dimensions. Madeleine Vionnet encourage les femmes à s'enorgueillir de proportions harmonieuses, du

beau dessin d'une poitrine ferme et ne pas honteuse, et de hanches bien galbées en leur finesse.'

5. 'Le rectangle d'étoffe, lorsqu'il est bien approprié, fait mieux ressortir la forme humaine. Les angles forment des parties excédantes qui retombent et s'étagent d'elles-mêmes en chutes et en sinuosités, donnant au corps un cadre de l'effet le plus heureux, un accompagnement brillant et riche, mais sans superfluité.'

6. See Drier (1987) for a perceptive review of the exhibition referred to in (1) above.

7. Her life is catalogued, with extensive photographs, in Charles-Roux (1981).

8. For a discussion of the relationship of dandyism to modernism see Lubbock (1983, p. 43).

9. For a discussion of Poiret's work in the context of orientalism and early modernism see Wollen (1987, p. 7).

10. See Baudelaire's discussion of the dandy in *The Painter of Modern Life* (Baudelaire, 1981).

11. Schiaparelli wrote in her autobiography that a contemporary press headline declared 'Schiaparelli collection enough to cause crisis in vocabulary' (Schiaparelli, 1954, p. 72).

12. Flügel (1930) discusses the displacement of interest from the body to clothes in Chapter 1 of *The Psychology of Clothes*.

13. 'Pour nous "Schiap" c'est beaucoup plus qu'une affaire de chiffons: à travers la costume elle a exprimé un défi aux conventions esthétiques, à une epoque où la couture risquait de se pèrdre dans less subtilités anémiques.'

14. For a discussion of the work of women artists in Surrealism see Chadwick (1985a).

15. In psychoanalytic theory fetishism is defined as a practice in which some inappropriate part of the body or an object, usually of clothing, is chosen as the object of sexual desire. The fetish object is always a symbol of the phallus. For both sexes the having or not having of the penis is a matter for anxiety which the fetish is chosen to reassure.

16. Whitney Chadwick suggests that Giacometti first encouraged Oppenheim to produce some fashion accessories and jewellery for Schiaparelli (Chadwick, 1985a, p. 122).

7. MAKING FASHION: TWO DESIGNERS

VIVIENNE WESTWOOD: 'MY STIMULUS IS ALWAYS ACADEMIC'[1]

Westwood looks to culture and to history: putting them together she makes fashion. She constructs a polemic of dress which is sometimes batty, sometimes schizoid, but always acute. Although her practice challenges many of the conventions of the fashion industry she has been an inspiration both to young contemporary designers and, more intriguingly, copied by very orthodox Parisian *couturiers*.

She has no formal training in fashion (she was originally a schoolteacher), and claims she learnt to cut by taking apart and copying original Teds' draped jackets. She started with her partner Malcolm McLaren, making and selling clothes from their shop in the King's Road, Let It Rock, in 1971. In 1976 they determined the look of punk from the shop, by then renamed Sex.[2] The Bondage collection of this period, and the obscene T-shirts (for which Westwood and McLaren were prosecuted), are in many ways exemplary of Westwood's approach. She tends to start with research. For the Bondage collection she examined the private world of fetishistic and sado-masochistic dress: 'I had to ask myself, why this extreme form of dress? Not that I strapped myself up and had sex like that. But on the other hand I also didn't just want to liberally *understand* why people did it. I wanted to get hold of those extreme articles of clothing and feel what it was like to wear them' (Westwood, quoted Ash, 1980).

On the basis of such 'research' Westwood creates fashion by changing the meanings of the garments she reclaims or recycles. Her methods produce clothes as objects which do not 'fit', which have been cut adrift from their familiar or symbolic place. In the punk Bondage collection of 1976, the straps and chains associated with private and perverse sexual practices were put on the street as elements within a different language of subcultural style. The sado-masochistic meanings of the articles then began to shift in a way that made the original significance of bondage clothes almost reassuring, at least familiar. Westwood's approach then is exploratory: 'The bondage clothes were ostensibly restricting but when you put them on they gave you a feeling of freedom. They made you want to move your arms around' (Westwood, quoted Ash, ibid.). Westwood was aware of the implications of cultural subversion in her practice. In 1977 the shop was renamed Seditionaries: 'For example, the word "Seditionaries" which I used to rename the shop, has always meant to me the necessity to *seduce* people into revolt . . .' (Westwood, quoted Ash, ibid.).

Westwood's collaboration with Malcolm McLaren in the punk period certainly seemed like a hard act to follow but the Pirate collection of 1981–2 was born out of the same combination of research, observation and a strategically anarchic approach to dress. In this collection Westwood engaged with the idea of cut, both in theory and in practice:

> When I did the Pirate collection I'd seen a picture of a man whose trousers were too big and they were all kind of rumpled around the crutch and all the pockets were baggy. I wanted to do that, but I couldn't pull that trouser off until I found a book which showed how people made breeches in those days and I found that the shape of trousers was quite, quite different . . . I wanted that rakish look of clothes which didn't fit, and I was into that for quite a long time, and I splurged off a whole thing of English *terrible* cutting.
>
> (Westwood, quoted *Blitz*, 41, May 1986)

The Pirate collection made the break with the punk repertoire. It was defiantly decorative, evoking a flamboyant and romantic past, a wild historical pageant. It was popularized by Adam and the Ants and later by Bow Wow Wow. During Westwood's collaboration with McLaren her work in fashion was galvanized by the association with the rock world. The original Bondage collection had been worn by the Sex Pistols and the Buffalo collection of 1982 appeared in the pop videos for McLaren's own recordings. The Pirate collection embodied the postmodern practice of using history as an image bank to be raided. However, it was more than fancy dress. It was structurally anarchic, as is all Westwood's work, and, like the Bondage collection, it made meanings out of its references to an outlawed group – pirates and sexual 'deviants' are both outcasts. The associations with law-breaking were particularly striking when the costumes were worn by very young girls (Plate 41).

Fashion has frequently 'fashionalized' folk costume, showing a tendency to sentimentalize the borrowed clothes. Where Westwood has borrowed from Third World cultures or from European history, the reworked garments and motifs retain their significance as anti-fashion. Her reworking manages to maintain dress as the site of a struggle between different readings. Fashion is located as the place in which the meaning of dress is revitalized rather than the place in which it is endlessly debunked. When she borrows from history Westwood indicates a sense of the significance of real time by subverting it.

In 1980 the name of the shop changed again, to World's End. It was fitted out with a topsy-turvy interior and a clock that ran backwards. In Westwood's work historical time and fashion's arbitrary and capricious sense of time are articulated as distinct phenomena that have become inextricably confused.

In 1981 Westwood, like Comme des Garçons, showed in Paris for the first time. The non-conformism of her Buffalo, Hobo, Witches and Punk Couture (also known as Punkature) collections was highlighted by the context of Parisian *couture*. The Buffalo collection (Plate 42) featured, for women, huge overskirts worn over padded underskirts, arranged to expose the multiple waistbands. This unfashionable kind of bulk was worn with falling down stockings and an upholstered satin bra that went over the layers of clothing.

Largely mud-coloured, the Buffalo look was inspired by the dress of Peruvian women, 'big women . . . who live in a space of their own, waiting for the world to grow up' (Westwood, quoted *Observer Colour Supplement*, 5 December 1982). The type of bra Westwood used was old-fashioned, a pre-'liberation' bra. She took the respectable, even matronly, underwear of white Western womanhood, and changed it into a fashion accessory. She claims to have been inspired by pictures of African tribesmen who recycled Western accessories as elements in their own, separate scheme of adornment. Of punk, she said: 'Safety pins definitely had an analogy in Third World culture, like putting feathers in your hair . . . or people in Africa who made necklaces out of old car hub caps' (Westwood quoted *i-D*, 33, February 1986).

In her approach to the appropriation and recycling of the cultural and industrial effluence of the West, Westwood articulated a contemporary and postmodern theme in fashion: the demise of European cultural supremacy. The Hobo collection was uniformly frayed, tattered and torn, provocatively so, in view of the garments' status as high fashion. As early as the Bondage collection she had been selling torn T-shirts – an early example of the attack against the ethics of production and consumption implicit in her work, where the breaking of sartorial codes articulates an oppositional stance.

When the collaboration with McLaren ceased, Westwood's subversive tactics became less clearly aggressive and more oblique, yet her work continued to act like a depth charge on the fashion world. She began to speak less of anarchy and more of an idea of womanliness and the body. 'I got tired of looking at clothes from the point of view of rebellion – I found it exhausting, and after a while I wasn't sure if I was right . . . That's why me and Malcolm separated, because I'm not so concerned with attacking . . . I'm more concerned with jumping over' (Westwood, quoted *i-D*, 33, February, 1986).

In 1985 she produced the mini-crini (Plate 43), a short hooped underskirt or skirt worn with a jacket or blazer and platform shoes. Ostensibly flying in the face of every practical advance in women's clothing, the silhouette was nevertheless widely plagiarized. Typically, Westwood's imitators borrowed the general look without the *idea*, the academicism that galvanizes her work. The mini-crini re-presents a consideration of the history of sexuality and of fashion's changing definition of the female body. The hooped crinoline is an invention of the nineteenth century, associated with empire, while the mini is a product of the 1960s and swinging London. It is a cultural hybrid that required to be read in terms of both its antecedents. If the crinoline stands in for a mythology of restriction and encumbrance in women's dress, in the mini-crini that mythology is juxtaposed with an equally dubious mythology of liberation associated with the mini-skirt. In it two sets of ideas about female desirability are conflated: one about covering, the other about uncovering the female body.

Westwood is clearly attracted to any form of dress that is 'outcast'. Victorian women's dress, particularly the crinoline and corset, has come to stand for an oppressive past as regards women's dress. In terms of a sartorial mythology these garments evoke a combination of tyranny and moralism that is repugnant to twentieth-century views of both women and fashion.[3] Westwood picks out garments such as the crinoline because they are anathematized, in the same way as bondage wear. However, unlike the nineteenth-century corset, the crinoline has not been

41. The shop assistant as outlaw: assistant at Seditionaries wearing clothes from Westwood and McLaren's Pirate collection, autumn/winter 1981–2. Photograph by Ted Polhemus

overworked in the twentieth century as a fetishized object. As the perfect anachronism, Westwood saw in the crinoline 'a sort of vitality that has never been exploited' (*i-D*, 45, March 1987) . The nineteenth-century crinoline exhibits the sheer perversity of dress, a perversity which has been denied within the rhetoric of twentieth-century functionalism. Nevertheless, Westwood's crinoline was worn without a corset and, in defiance of its reputation as an impractical garment, hers was 'easy' to wear. She claimed to have bicycled in hers and said 'when you sit down it just collapses around you, so you don't even notice it' (Westwood, quoted *i-D*, 33, February 1986).

Nevertheless, in terms of its 'academicism' the mini-crini makes reference to the encumbrance of Victorian women's clothes. Westwood insists both on the ponderous regality of the crinoline and on its eroticism: 'The crinolines are very, very sexy, there was never a fashion *invented* that was more sexy, especially in the big Victorian form. How great to come into a room and occupy six feet of space or have chairs invented for you. The mini-crinoline moves and sways, constantly revealing areas of flesh. Sometimes it's quite stiff and sometimes it's really wiggly, depending on the fabric. It's perfect for summer but it's like being naked in winter. I suppose I should make something to go underneath it for when it gets cold. But female *goodness*, I'm not sure.' (Westwood, quoted *i-D*, 45, March 1987). Here is a deliberate challenge to the functionalist understanding of dress and an invitation to open up or re-read the meaning of dress of the past, specifically women's dress.

For Westwood fashion is a discourse that works through excess, eccentricity and paradox. The mini-crini might be read as an embodiment of contradiction. It combines opposing ideologies of femininity which are manifested in terms of dress as encumbrance, covering, liberation, revelation. In addition the crinoline itself is contradictory. In the nineteenth century, women wearing the crinoline were made supremely visible at the same time as they were symbolically immobilized.[4] Paradoxically, this symbolic immobilization was accompanied by a greater freedom of movement conferred by the hooped crinoline, which replaced the heavy petticoats previously used to give fullness to the skirt. The crinoline was part of the overblown opulence of Empire; its formalization represented solidity and conformity, yet it was also part of the sub-plot of nineteenth-century female dress in which concealment, secrecy and wrapping became a form of sexual display.

In the mid nineteenth century the difference between male and female dress became polarized, particularly in terms of silhouette. The combination of corset and crinoline emphasized bosom and waist. At the same time as the corset restricted the

42. The Buffalo Gal: layers of bulky clothing worn with a satin bra on top. Westwood and McLaren's Buffalo collection of autumn/winter 1982–3. Photograph by Chris Woode

female form

waist, the crinoline sketched the hips in an over-large gesture in a period when women's child-bearing role was highly valued. The implicit association of the huge skirt with maternal fecundity becomes explicit in Westwood's version: 'For the last ten years clothes have had shoulder pads and tight hips – that's supposed to be the sexy look, the inverted triangle – but I think people want a more feminine fitting. Women want to be strong, but in a feminine way' (Westwood, quoted *i-D*, 33, February 1986). At the same time the maternal associations of the crinoline are countered by those of the mini – anti-maternal, even infantile. As a hybrid the mini-crini invites speculation on the cultural definition of the female body.

The nineteenth-century crinoline, often represented as static, immobile, concealing and respectable, was also dynamic, spectacular and erotic. Westwood recoups something of this quality and with it the essential perversity of the crinoline. The crinoline is an 'adult' garment that somehow also incorporates the buffoonery of childhood and play. It is an historical curiosity riddled with contradictory or secret sexual meanings, redolent of the dark ages of Victorian life. Westwood communicates a sense of historical curiosity in her work, a sense of the way in which dress gives us 'clues' to the secret, unspoken or forgotten meanings of the body. Her practice is comparable to a child 'investigating' adult garments, rummaging through the historical wardrobe. In its approach to cultural history Westwood's practice could be compared to the psychoanalytic process in which the landscape of the past begins to shift inexorably as it is spoken in the present.

The crinoline's identification with Empire and regality are not only recognized but also embraced by Westwood in her preoccupation with royalty and dumpy aristocracy, a specific instance of her perennial theme of national identity and English history. The mini-crini was worn with 'little coats like the Queen wears . . . like I used to wear when I was a child' (Westwood, quoted *i-D*, 33, February 1986). Her 1987 collection for women featured boarding-school clothes with fake ermine jackets, tiny riding hats and tweeds (Plate 44). She appeared on a television chat show in a crown made of Harris tweed. In contrast to her earlier, anti-establishment poses the collection suggested an identification with the Queen as the benign Great Mother, a curious revival of middle-class Victorian mother worship centred around the royal mother. Yet transgression and conformity became mixed here, in a deceptively simple homage to the powerful mother which was more than the obeisance of the good daughter or the loyal subject. Westwood's Royal collection provided an alternative version of fashion influenced by the British Royal Family. Rather than humbly aspiring to the glamour of Princess Diana, young women could

43. Academic fashion: Vivienne Westwood's original mini-crini, spring/summer 1986.
Photograph by Andrew Macpherson, styling by Amanda Grieve, from *i–D*, 33, February 1986

sport a tweed crown and fake ermine tippet. To identify with the Queen is presumptuous; to dress up like her is to forget your place. The fact that the Queen's clothes have traditionally been reviled in the fashion world as lacking in style and sex appeal also marks them out as yet more fertile ground for Westwood's strategic play on the interrelated themes of Englishness and class. In terms of these concerns there is a direct link between the punk Bondage collection of 1976 and the Royal collection of 1987. At one point the clothes in the World's End shop bore the label 'Born in England'.

There is a driving force behind Westwood's manipulation of the cultural meanings of clothes. In all her interviews she talks of 'sexiness' in relation to women and fashion: 'I've never thought it powerful to be like a second-rate man. Femininity is stronger, and I don't understand why people keep plugging this boring asexual body. At my age I'd rather have a bit of flab, I actually think that's more sexy. I *like* my own body' (Westwood, quoted *i-D*, 45, March 1987). For Westwood, 'sexiness' is not the straightforward attribute that fashion so often presents it as, but a matter for enquiry, exploration and debate, even for improvisation.

All her work pivots around the idea of a sexuality which is autonomous and subjectively defined. When she talks of what is 'sexy' the stress is on what will *feel* sexy to the wearer, so that the issue becomes one of the wearer's libido, rather than one of 'being attractive'. Westwood fosters the idea of a self-defined feminine libido, however demented, which communicates itself idiosyncratically through dress. The 'madness' of her women's clothes partly consists in the madness of that project: a feminine sexuality working outside the law, outside the constraints of male definition. The sexiness she expounds is autonomous: if the wearer *thinks* it is sexy, then it is. Such a position comes close to a kind of sartorial psychosis that has particularly transgressive meanings for women.

The idea of autonomy in relation to women's clothes is transgressive in itself. In Westwood's work the theme of autonomy and control central to male dandyism re-emerges for women as, paradoxically, ordered around disorder. The disorderly woman and the dandy, the pirate and the sexual deviant, are all 'outside the law' (Baudelaire, 1981, p. 419). Her emphasis on culture, history and sexuality demonstrates that sexuality has a history, that it can change in a way which opens up possibilities in the present. Further, she suggests fashion as the communicator of those possibilities: 'Fashion is such an immediate form of communication. It does get its results really quickly. People can take it and feel it' (Westwood, quoted *Blitz*, 41, May 1986).

44. Vivienne Westwood in her version of the royal wardrobe. The photograph appeared in *i–D* magazine where the original artwork had the words 'Viv rules UK!' graffitied next to the image. Photograph by Ben Westwood

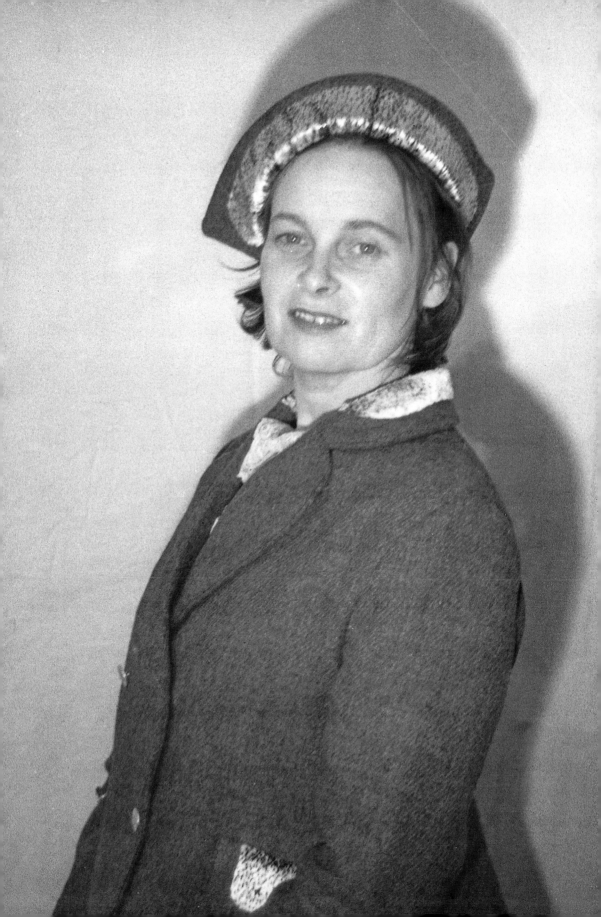

REI KAWAKUBO; 'I START FROM ZERO'[5]

If Vivienne Westwood works with time, history and culture Rei Kawakubo appears to avoid these references in her work. Often extreme, her designs for women have a distinction and a dignity that is a function of Kawakubo's respect for materials and for the wholeness of the body. In these terms her work might usefully be compared to that of Vionnet. While she avoids polemic there is a fine calculation in the way in which Kawakubo positions her contemplative and sculptural work within the frenzy of contemporary Western fashion.

Rei Kawakubo is a Japanese designer with no formal training in fashion. She was born in 1942 in Tokyo and graduated from Tokyo Keio University in 1964 with a degree in Aesthetics. She then worked in the advertising department of a textile manufacturer. She started making clothes because when styling advertisements she could not find the sort of garments she wanted. From 1966 she worked as a freelance stylist for seven years before starting her own company, Comme des Garçons. Like Vivienne Westwood she designs for both sexes; this discussion of her work, however, focuses on her clothes for women. Kawakubo has produced extraordinary innovations of cut, detailing and fabric. Yet her clothes, for all their cleverness, never become mere puzzles. On the body the intelligence of their design works to articulate the effectiveness of the body itself. The body gives form to the clothes, the clothes articulate the body.

Like Madeleine Vionnet, Rei Kawakubo is a cloth designer, who starts from the fabric itself, with a strong sense of the feel of the garment. Kawakubo's clothes are not obviously sensuous in the way Vionnet's often are, but they change the parameters of the wearer's body, the sense of where the edges of the body are, where it meets the space around it. Even in the more tailored clothes (Plates 47 and 48) the fabrics are allowed to move, and to move with the body. Indeed, without movement, the clothes are only half what they might be: the body in motion reveals their form and structure and sets off the qualities of the fabric. Movement becomes a component of her design, as light may be in architcture; she wants to make 'clothes where the body can move freely' (Kawakubo, quoted *Women's Wear Daily*, 1 March 1983). Kawakubo's clothes are constructed in anticipation of movement. The body's movement releases the potential of the garment. As the wearer moves unexpected features of cut are revealed in odd places. In this sense the wearer is also the maker of the garment.

With the Wrapped collection (Plate 45), each garment permitted a multiplicity of wearings. The final act in making the garment is performed by the wearer who chooses which opening to put her head through and how to wrap or tie the flaps or appendages of material. Within the unusualness of her clothes is a calculated refusal to be prescriptive; she communicates a respect for the body and for the autonomy and intelligence of the wearer. She is a reductionist designer. As she pares down a garment, decorating by making holes rather than by adding in the form of appliqué or embroidery, functional considerations are transcended. Many of the garments in the early collections had one arm longer than the other, or two holes for the head. Paradoxically, their anti-functionalism made them comfortable, easy to move in. In these earlier collections she questioned the logic of clothing itself. By displacing a sleeve, lowering one armhole, or making an amorphous black jersey garment that could be worn as a belt, hat or scarf she drew attention to the materiality of the garment itself, to its own logic which one takes for granted. In her early collections many of the clothes were torn, wrapped and swathed (Plate 45), with sleeves extruded in unexpected places and then wrapped round the body. Kawakubo broke the canons of *couture* yet she chose to show in Paris. The presentation of the first Paris show was startlingly different from anything that had gone before: dramatic lighting flickered on and off, black-clad models stalked across the catwalk, discordant music stopped and started. The fashion press responded by calling her work Japan's answer to the atom bomb, dubbing it the post-holocaust look and, possibly more insulting in its own terms, the bag-lady look.

Plate 46 shows a piece from the Elastic collection of 1983. The piece has elasticated holes in the top which is worn over a similarly elasticated undergarment. Huge openings in the garment only reveal another garment beneath. In both garments the wearer has a choice of which hole to put her arms and head through. She can thus drape it differently, and position the 'spare' holes as desired. The Wrapped collection (Plate 45) and the Elastic collection (Plate 46) were received unfavourably by some; the American fashion press in particular condemned them as unsexy. Kawakubo's response has been to assert that one does not rely on one's clothes to be sexy but on oneself. In Kawakubo's work, as in Westwood's, the meaning of 'sexiness' in relation to women's clothes and fashion is questioned, although with very different results. Westwood has said (in reference to her pornographic T-shirts of the punk period), 'I hate innuendo' (Ash, 1980). Kawakubo's work also eschews innuendo where that suggests teasing or titillation. Although she has designed garments which reveal parts of the body through unexpected vents or holes, they are parts of the body that have, as it were, no names:

45. Questioning the logic of clothing: Comme des Garçons' Wrapped collection, 1983.
Photograph by Hans Feurer, courtesy of Comme des Garçons

the inside of the knee, a section of the ribcage, or the lower back revealed by an oblong window. Equally, garments may gape only to reveal another layer of fabric beneath. All this challenges the vocabulary of 'sexiness' in women's fashion: a 'hint' of this, a 'flattering glimpse' of that, clothes with 'plunging necklines', clothes which are 'frankly feminine', 'body hugging' and 'clinging'.

In 1982–3 Kawakubo designed a collection based on dark blue skirts and pinafores worn with white blouses. The clothes, absolutely simple although structurally innovative, were remininiscent of girls' school uniforms but managed to achieve a heroic gracefulness, avoiding the *louche* overtones associated with grown-up women wearing schoolgirls' clothes. This collection in particular emphasized a purposefulness in her work. Kawakubo's clothes rely on aplomb, grace and strength of movement; they are serious while never being boring. There is a purity in Kawakubo's work that is never rhetorical.

While the body's capacity for movement is foregrounded in her work, the emphasis on movement is not especially sporty nor does it insist on practicality. If these clothes ask anything of the wearer it is that she be in charge, that she wear the clothes rather than be worn by them. In deciding how to wear them she decides how to move. Westwood's dictum 'what your body can do physically is what you're about' (Westwood, quoted *Observer Colour Supplement*, 5 December 1982) stands for Kawakubo's work too. Where Westwood, in the Bondage work, cut off possibilities of movement in order to articulate them, Kawakubo's work suggests freedom of movement by highlighting the capacities of the fabric and the wearer's choices in relation to the garment.

Like Westwood's, Kawakubo's work may be read as a meditation on 'sexiness' and what it is about. Both designers foreground the issue of the body's movement in relation to dress. In Kawakubo's designs for women eroticism is a function of undoing the clichés about the body. When working with the female body 'starting from zero' amounts to a 'making strange' and in this way Kawakubo allows one to 're-see' the body and its possibilities. Emphasizing the continuity of the female body, even its contiguity, in space, calls into question the practice of 'seeing the body in bits' that has been identified as intrinsic to the representation of the female body in patriarchal culture. This fragmentation is a central term in Western fashion's representations of women's bodies. Crucially, as Kawakubo demonstrates, seeing the body whole is never simple: it produces in her work a representation of the body that is always demanding, complex and sophisticated. Kawakubo achieves more than the mere denial of a stereotype of femininity. To

46. Commes des Garçons' Elastic collection, 1986. The wearer chooses how to put on two similar garments, one over the other, and where to dispose the spare holes. Photograph by Peter Lindbergh, courtesy of Comme des Garçons

rearticulate the body through clothing as she does is to effect a shift in the hierarchy of meanings ascribed to the bodily parts. The traditionally sexy is jettisoned in favour of something less determined, in favour, perhaps, of pleasure, and in particular the wearer's pleasure.

'Starting from zero' suggests the minimalism that is a part of Kawakubo's practice, especially in the earlier collections. In many ways Kawakubo's design practice is deliberately analogous to a fine art practice. There is a coherence to her thinking which works against the changing demands of fashion. Like Vionnet, Kawakubo decontextualized her early work from the polemics of fashion where that revolved around contemporaneity. Yet she remained at the head of the avant-garde in women's fashion. Like Vionnet, too, Kawakubo starts with the fabric. Vionnet draped, designed in the round. She had fabric woven double width for her bias-cut dresses. Kawakubo starts with the yarn, all of which is woven in her factory. In the early 1980s the inherent qualities of fabrics were made a feature of her work. Her fabrics were experimented with. They might be washed and left out in the sun, or left to dry in a crumpled heap. She was the first to use crumpled linen, previously considered a material that required immaculate pressing. In her early collections she used subtle vegetable dyes. The resulting cloth was already imbued with features that were never extraneous to the finished garment. One reason why her clothes were so expensive was that one piece of fabric may have taken many days to produce and have passed through many pairs of hands. This sensitivity to materials militates against a mechanical perfection:

The machines that make fabric are more and more making uniform, flawless textures. I like it best when something is off – not perfect. Hand weaving is the best way to achieve this. Since this isn't always possible, we loosen a screw of the machines here and there so they can't do exactly what they're supposed to do.

(Kawakubo, quoted Koren, 1985, p. 117)

Similarly in her early work she used both Western smocking and Japanese *sashiko*,[6] both peasant techniques used in working clothes. More recently Kawakubo has engaged with synthetic fabrics, particularly rayon, and with the production of new ones. Again, the way in which she deals with them suggests a phenomenological approach to materials. Designing in rayon, a discredited material, she demonstrates what rayon can do, how it behaves, in the same way as she will explore the quality of

47. A torrent of Japanese tartan. A Comme des Garçons' suit of 1986 which combines tailored and draped elements. Photograph by Peter Lindbergh, courtesy of Comme des Garçons

cotton. At the same time, dealing with man-made fibres is symptomatic of the shift in her work in the mid 1980s towards an engagement with the stuff of culture as opposed to the stuff of nature. However, in both cases her approach is characterized by 'starting from zero', by starting with the yarn.

The work from the early 1980s was voluminous, often baggy, and dark. She has been quoted as saying, 'I work in three shades of black.' Nevertheless, she always used colour with a subtlety which the statement suggests. She and Yohji Yamamoto were responsible for a drastic change in high-street fashion in the early to mid 1980s when their influence filtered through to the high-street shops. However, by the mid 1980s she was cutting closer to the body. In this work she engaged with tailoring and fit as formal ideas without using them in conventional ways. For example, dresses which at first appeared far more conventional than her earlier work in fact had asymmetrical fins or pouches sewn into the skirt which were revealed when the wearer walked. This engagement with tailoring and fit as opposed to drapery and wrapping is an extension in her work of her approach to clothes as cultural objects.

Plate 47 shows a suit in which tailoring and drapery appear together. It is almost as if the orthodoxies of the suit are subverted by the torrent of 'Japanese tartan' drapery which escapes from under the jacket. The drapery can be thrown over the shoulder like a plaid. A feature of her fitted suits of the mid 1980s was the way in which fabric was made to work in several ways on one body, sometimes within one garment. Cutting material to fit the body and letting it 'go' in the same piece suggests the interaction of the cultural with the natural in a way which parallels the relation of the body to dress. Part of the sophistication of her work is the way in which it is able to rearticulate the body at the heart of culture's pre-eminent discourse of artificiality, fashion.

The Bonded dress of 1986 (Plate 48) was a departure of a different kind. Black cotton, rayon and polyurethane are bonded together in a dress with a tulip skirt that falls clear of the line of the body. Its shape abstracts and echoes that of the hips. Like a shell the hem spirals up, gesturing towards a length of skirt while becoming a feature in itself. It is interesting to compare this piece to Westwood's mini-crini; there is a similarity in the concerns of the two designers although they are played out in quite different ways. Kawakubo investigates the body and its relation to clothes from the starting point of form while Westwood works with metaphor, reference and argument. In the dress in Plate 48 the skirt is structured to keep its form independently of the body in contrast to the relation between body and dress in the earlier work (Plates 45 and 46). Nevertheless the piece does not ignore

48. Organic tailoring: black cotton, rayon and polyurethane bonded dress by Comme des Garçons, 1986. Photograph by Steven Meisel, courtesy of Comme des Garçons

the body but makes palpable the space around it. Despite its appearance the dress is not stiff but flexible and dynamic. The emphasis on structure refers both to the engineering of dress and to organic forms. It incorporates the full skirt of Western women's dress but its unfamiliar contours suggest a garment that is not of the West.

How such a garment is read perhaps changes depending on where one is in the world. Working within Western fashion with an approach to clothes which is not confined by Western codes, Kawakubo has opened up new perspectives in fashion. Westwood, through her preoccupation with 'England', uses cultural particularities to make reference to a global space without losing the perspective of history. Kawakubo constructs garments that engage with cultural difference and with its articulation in dress at a formal level. She has appropriated Western fashion and its history as a discourse among other discourses about dress. Her practice suggests a new possibility in fashion: exploring the meanings fashion makes with the body, she is simultaneously working within a conception and experience of cultural difference.

FOOTNOTES

1. Vivienne Westwood, quoted *The Face*, 9, January 1981.
2. Less emphasis is placed on Sex and the Bondage collection here as they are dealt with in Chapter 2, 'Women and Punk: a case history'.
3. These views were challenged in David Kunzle's book *Fashion and Fetishism: a Social History of the Corset, Tight-Lacing and Other Forms of Body Sculpture in the West* (Kunzle, 1980), and further debated by Valerie Steele in *Fashion and Eroticism: Ideals of Feminine Beauty from the Victorian Era to the Jazz Age* (Steele, 1985).
4. In *The Theory of the Leisure Class*, written in 1899, Thorstein Veblen, argued that the encumbrance of Victorian women's dress spoke their inability to do useful work. The opulence of their dress, he argued, proclaimed their obligation to consume, vicariously, for the head of the household (Veblen, 1953, Chapter 7).
5. Kawakubo, quoted *Women's Wear Daily*, USA, 1 March 1983.
6. *Sashiko* is a traditional technique whereby worn-out indigo work clothes are stitched together with little white running stitches to form a new garment. It is a 'poor' technique used by rural workers and fishermen.

AFTERWORD

. . . and like logic fashion is stripped of content, but not of meaning. A kind of machine for maintaining meaning without ever fixing it, it is forever a disappointed meaning, but it is nevertheless a meaning: without content, it then becomes the spectacle human beings grant themselves of their power to make the insignificant signify.

Roland Barthes (1915–80)

One had as good be out of the world, as out of the fashion.

Colly Cibber (1671–1757)

Moreover the Lord saith, Because the daughters of Zion are haughty, and walk with stretched-forth necks and wanton eyes, walking and mincing as they go, and making a tinkling with their feet: Therefore the Lord will smite with a scab the crown of the head of the daughters of Zion, and the Lord will discover their secret parts. In that day the Lord will take away the bravery of their tinkling ornaments about their feet, and their cauls, and their round tires like the moon, The chains, and the bracelets, and the mufflers, The bonnets, and the ornaments of the legs, and the headbands, and the tablets and the earrings, The rings and nose jewels,

The changeable suits of apparel, and the mantles, and the wimples, and the crisping pins, The glasses, and the fine linen, and the hoods, and the veils. And it shall come to pass that instead of sweet smell there shall be stink; and instead of a girdle a rent; and instead of well-set hair baldness; and instead of a stomacher a girding of sackcloth; and burning instead of beauty.

Isaiah, 3:16–24

There's no such thing as a moral dress . . . it's people who are moral or immoral.

Jennie Churchill (1854–1921)

Delight in Disorder

A sweet disorder in the dress
Kindles in clothes a wantonness:
A lawn about the shoulders thrown
Into a fine distraction:
An evening lace, which here and there
Enthrals the crimson stomacher:
A cuff neglectful, and thereby
Ribbands to flow confusedly:
A winning wave, deserving note,
In the tempestuous petticoat:
A careless shoe-string, in whose tie
I see a wild civility:
Do more bewitch me than when art
Is too precise in every part.

Robert Herrick (1591–1674)

The dress of women goes even further than that of men in the way of demonstrating the wearer's abstinence from productive employment. It needs no argument to enforce the generalization that the more elegant styles of feminine bonnets go even farther towards making work impossible than does the man's high hat. The woman's shoe adds the so-called French heel to the evidence of enforced leisure afforded by its polish; because this high heel obviously makes any, even the simplest and most necessary manual work extremely difficult. The like is true even in a higher degree of the skirt and the rest of the drapery which characterizes woman's dress. The substantial reason for our tenacious attachment to the skirt is just this: it is expensive and it hampers the wearer at every turn and incapacitates her for all useful exertion. The like is true of the feminine custom of wearing the hair excessively long.

Thorstein Veblen (1857–1929)

To a woman, the consciousness of being well-dressed gives a sense of tranquillity that religion fails to bestow.

Helen Olcott Bell (1830–1918)

When one fails to adhere to an accepted code one becomes an insurgent. A woman who dresses in an outlandish manner lies when she affirms with an air of simplicity that she dresses to suit herself, nothing more. She knows perfectly well that to suit herself is to be outlandish.

Simone de Beauvoir (1908–86)

I always wear slacks because of the brambles and maybe the snakes.

Katharine Hepburn (1909–   )

Sources

Barthes, Roland, 1985, *The Fashion System*, Jonathan Cape, p. 288
Partner, Elaine (ed.), 1987, *The Quotable Woman*, Anchor Books, pp. 56, 92, 318
Oxford Dictionary of Quotations, 3rd ed. 1980, OUP, p. 151
The New Oxford Book of English Verse, 1972, OUP, p. 240
Veblen, Thorstein, 1953, *The Theory of the Leisure Class*, Viking Press, NY, p. 121
de Beauvoir, Simone, 1972, *The Second Sex*, Penguin Books, p. 692

BIBLIOGRAPHY

The place of publication is London, unless otherwise stated.

Ackroyd, Peter, 1979, *Dressing Up. Tranvestism and Drag: The History of an Obsession*, Thames & Hudson

Ash, Juliet, 1980, 'Sex is fashion is Sex: an interview with Vivienne Westwood', *ZG*, No. 2

Barthes, Roland, 1984, *Camera Lucida*, Fontana

Barthes, Roland, 1985, *The Fashion System*, Jonathan Cape

Baudelaire, Charles, 1981, 'The Painter of Modern Life', *Selected Writings on Art and Artists*, Cambridge University Press

Baudrillard, Jean, 1983, *Simulations*, Semiotext(e), New York

Benjamin, Walter, 1976, *Charles Baudelaire: A Lyric Poet in the Era of High Capitalism*, Verso Editions

Benthall, Jonathan and Polhemus, Ted (eds), 1975, *The Body as a Medium of Expression*, Allen Lane

Berger, John, 1972, *Ways of Seeing*, BBC Publications and Penguin Books

Bertin, Célia, 1956, *Paris à la Mode*, Victor Gollancz

Betterton, Rosemary (ed), 1987, *Looking On: Images of Femininity in the Visual Arts and Media*, Pandora

Brooks, Rosetta, 1980, 'Fashion: Double Page Spread', *Camerawork*, No. 17

Brooks, Rosetta, 1981, 'Sighs and Whispers in Bloomingdales', *Camerawork*, No. 3

Burgin, V., Donald, J., Kaplan, C. (eds), 1986, *Formations of Fantasy*, Methuen

Burgin, Victor, 1986, 'Diderot, Barthes, *Vertigo*', *Formations of Fantasy*, Methuen. Also in Burgin, Victor, 1986, *The End of Art Theory: Criticism and Postmodernity*, Macmillan

Carter, Ernestine, 1977, *The Changing World of Fashion*, Weidenfeld & Nicolson

Carter, Angela, 1982, 'The Wound in the Face', *Nothing Sacred: Selected Writings*, Virago

Carter, Angela, 1982, 'The Bridled Sweeties', *Nothing Sacred: Selected Writings*, Virago

Chadwick, Whitney, 1985a, *Women Artists in the Surrealist Movement*, Thames & Hudson

Chadwick, Whitney, 1985b, 'The Muse as Artist: Women in the Surrealist Movement', *Art in America*, July

Charles-Roux, Edmonde, 1982 paperback edition, *Chanel and her World*, Weidenfeld & Nicolson

Clark, T.J., 1980, 'Preliminaries to a Possible Treatment of "Olympia" in 1865', *Screen*, Vol. 21, No. 1

Clark, T.J., 1985, *The Painting of Modern Life*, Thames & Hudson

Colette, 1971, *The Pure and the Impure*, Penguin Books

Coward, Rosalind, 1984, *Female Desire*, Paladin Books

de Beauvoir, Simone, 1960, *Brigitte Bardot and the Lolita Syndrome*, André Deutsch and Weidenfeld & Nicolson

de Beauvoir, Simone, 1972, *The Second Sex*, Penguin Books

Doane, Mary Ann, 1982, 'Film and the Masquerade: Theorizing the Female Spectator', *Screen*, Vol. 23, No. 3–4

Drier, Deborah, 1987, 'Designing Women', *Art in America*, May

Eco, Umberto, 1986, *Faith in Fakes*, Secker & Warburg

Edwards, Janet Radcliffe, 1980, *The Sceptical Feminist*, Routledge & Kegan Paul

Fashion Institute of Technology, 1987, *Three Women: Madeleine Vionnet, Claire McCardell and Rei Kawakubo*, New York, 24 February–18 April

Flügel, J.C., 1930, *The Psychology of Clothes*, Hogarth Press

Garnier, Guillaume, 1984, *Hommage à Elsa Schiaparelli*, Ville de Paris, Musée de la Mode et du Costume, 21 Juin–30 Août

Ginsberg, M.B., 1975, *Fashion 1900–1939*, Scottish Arts Council and the Victoria and Albert Museum

Gombrich, E.H., 1960, *Art and Illusion: A Study in the Psychology of Pictorial Representation*, Phaidon

Hall, S., Clarke, J., Jefferson, T., Roberts, B. (eds), 1976, *Resistance Through Rituals*, Hutchinson

Hall-Duncan, Nancy, 1979, *The History of Fashion Photography*, Alpine Books Company, New York

Hamilton, George Heard, 1972 revised edition, *Painting and Sculpture in Europe: 1880–1940*, Pelican Books

Harrison, Martin, 1985, *Shots of Style*, Victoria and Albert Museum

Hebdige, Dick, 1979, *Subculture: The Meaning of Style*, Methuen

Heath, Stephen, 1986, 'Joan Rivière and the Masquerade' in Burgin, V., Donald, J., Kaplan, C. (eds), *Formations of Fantasy*, Methuen

Hollander, Anne, 1980, *Seeing Through Clothes*, Avon Books, USA

Jameson, Frederic, 1984, 'Postmodernism: The Cultural Logic of Late Capitalism', *New Left Review*, Vol. 146

Jencks, Charles, 1984 revised edition, *The Language of Post-Modern Architecture*, Academy Editions

König, René, 1973, *The Restless Image*, Allen & Unwin

Koren, Leonard, 1985, *New Fashion Japan*, Kodansha International, Tokyo, New York, San Francisco

Kytsis, Krystina, 1983, 'Icons of Glamour; Echoes of Death', *ZG*, no number

Kunzle, David, 1980, *Fashion and Fetishism: A Social History of the Corset, Tight-Lacing and Other Forms of Body Sculpture in the West*, Rowan & Littlefield, USA

Lubbock, Jules, 1983, 'Adolf Loos and the English Dandy', *Architectural Review*, Vol. CLXIX, No. 1038, August

Mapplethorpe, Robert, 1983, *Lady Lisa Lyon*, Viking Press, New York

McRobbie, Angela, 1980, 'Settling Accounts with Subculture', *Screen*, Vol. 34, No. 4

Moers, Ellen, 1960, *The Dandy: from Brummell to Beerbohm*, Secker & Warburg

Mitchell, Juliet, 1971, *Women's Estate*, Penguin Books

Morgan, Robin (ed), 1970, *Sisterhood is Powerful: An Anthology of Writings from the Women's Liberation Movement*, Vintage Books, Random House, New York

Mulvey, Laura, 1975, 'Visual Pleasure and Narrative Cinema', *Screen*, Vol. 16, No. 3

Mulvey, Laura, 1981, 'Afterthoughts on Visual Pleasure and Narrative Cinema, inspired by *Duel in the Sun* (King Vidor 1946)', *Framework*, 15/16/17, Summer

Myers, Kathy, 1982a, 'Fashion 'n' Passion', *Screen*, Vol. 23, No. 3–4. Reprinted in Betterton, 1987

Myers, Kathy, 1982b, 'Towards a Feminist Erotica', *Camerawork*, No. 24. Reprinted in Betterton, 1987, and in Robinson, 1987

Newton, Helmut, 1984, *World Without Men*, Quartet Books

Paz, Octavio, 1962, *The Labyrinth of Solitude*, Grove Press, New York

Penn, Irving, 1977, text by Vreeland, Diana, *Inventive Paris Clothes, 1909–1939*, Thames & Hudson, and Viking Press, New York

Polhemus, Ted and Proctor, Lynn, 1978, *Fashion and Anti-Fashion*, Thames & Hudson

Rimmer, Dave, 1985, *Like Punk Never Happened: Culture Club and the New Pop*, Faber & Faber

Rivière, Joan, 1986, 'Womanliness as a Masquerade', reprinted in Burgin, V., Donald, J., Kaplan, C. (eds), 1986, *Formations of Fantasy*, Methuen

Roach, Mary Ellen and Eichner, Joanne B. (eds), 1965, *Dress, Adornment and the Social Order*, John Wiley & Sons, New York

Robinson, Hilary (ed.), 1987, *Visibly Female*, Camden Press

Schiaparelli, Elsa, 1954, *Shocking Life*, Dent

Shottenkirk, Dena, 1983, 'Fashion Fictions: Absence and the Fast Heartbeat', *ZG*, No. 9, 'Breakdown' issue

Silverman, Kaja, 1986, 'Fragments of a Fashionable Discourse', in Modleski, Tania (ed.), 1986, *Studies in Entertainment*, Indiana University Press, USA

Steele, Valerie, 1985, *Fashion and Eroticism: Ideals of Feminine Beauty from the Victorian Era to the Jazz Age*, Oxford University Press

Steward, Sue and Garratt, Sheryl, 1984, *Signed, Sealed and Delivered: True Life Stories of Women in Pop*, Pluto Press

Turbeville, Deborah, 1978, *Wallflower*, Quartet Books

Veblen, Thorstein, 1953, *The Theory of the Leisure Class*, Viking Press, New York

Warhol, Andy, 1976, *From A to B and Back Again: The Philosophy of Andy Warhol*, Picador

Williamson, Judith, 1978, *Decoding Advertisements*, Marion Boyars

Williamson, Judith, 1983, 'Images of Women', *Screen*, Vol. 24, No. 6

Wilson, Elizabeth, 1985, *Adorned in Dreams*, Virago

Wollen, Peter, 1987, 'Fashion/orientalism/the body', *New Formations*, No. 1, Spring

Woolf, Virginia, 1942, *Orlando*, Penguin Books

INDEX